Brain Murmurings

Flashes of Insight and Other Southern Pearls

AILEEN ANN TOCE

Dedication

For my only son, Nicholas Domenic Toce, Richmond, VA, who inspired so many of my stories and gave me the title for the book. To all my girlfriends: Trish, Judy, Vivien, Sharon, Jude, Carla, Dottie, Susan, Debbie and Velma, whose love and support never wavered. Gratitude to my honey, Rick Franasiak, Glade Valley, NC, who has always loved every word I've ever written and worked tirelessly to organize a lifetime of my typed stories. To Ken Hall, Powder Springs, GA, without his early encouragement of my writing, I might have given up long ago; and to Tina Jordan, Sparta, NC, the friend who took my hand and guided me on the journey of publishing. A special thank you to Bob Bamburg, Editor of the Alleghany News, Sparta, NC, who gave me my first newspaper column and set my writer's voice free. His faith in me brought forth a writing confidence I didn't know I possessed. Gratitude to James Chandler, Sparta, NC, who gave me the name of my newspaper column, 'Thoughts To Ponder', and for his friendship that has meant so much. Thanks to each of you from the bottom of my heart. ~ Aileen Toce, 2022

Foreword

In my role as editor of a small-town newspaper, a lot of written material comes across my desk. Some is well written, but most is utilitarian - a notice of an upcoming meeting, an engagement announcement, a letter chiding a local politician. Rarely am I surprised. Aileen Toce surprised me.

She dropped off a manila envelope that sat on my desk for a day or two, waiting for me to find a spare moment to examine it. When that moment came, I was blown away. There was page after page of neatly typed essays reflecting on some aspect of life. It was not the subjects that were remarkable, but rather the description - the imagery she painted - and the insights she drew from everyday experiences.

There was a tempo to her writing. It seemed to inhabit a space between prose and poetry. It was heartfelt and each essay touched my heart in some way. Most filled the page, but some were barely half a page. I write a weekly column for the newspaper and struggle to say anything meaningful in less than 700 words. Aileen could move me to tears in half as many.

From the number of pages in that manila folder, I feared that she had said all she had to say. Not true. Her writing has been regularly featured on the pages of the newspaper since 2018, and she sends me new selections each week to choose from.

I am sure that you will be as engaged by her writing as I am.

Bob Bamburg, Editor, Alleghany News

INTRODUCTION

There are two things you need to know about this book before you dive in. First, the inspiration - it came from my son, Nicholas Toce. Years ago, I would ask him to read one of my short stories and to tell me what he thought. Once he said, "Mom, these aren't stories; they're brain murmurings." So I'm dedicating this book to him. He fills my heart, my thoughts, and a great many of my stories. He's there in the early stories, the later ones, and I'm sure the ones yet to come.

Second, I really can't take full credit for what you are about to read. You see, these thoughts, these flashes of insight, these stories - whatever you want to call them literally just pour out of me. Since childhood they come unbidden, usually at inconvenient times that send me scrambling for pen and pad, and I can barely write them down fast enough. If they are not captured immediately, they vanish and can not be retrieved. Through the years there have been months when nothing came. I have learned to live with this peculiarity. I know not where my stories come from nor why they come to me, but I do know I want to share them. Perhaps by word or phrase, they may help someone.

I live on a mountain in a cabin in the woods of North Carolina - God's country, doncha know. I spent years circling through life to get back here. In this place my heart is home; it soothes my soul and brings peace to my spirit. It allows my thoughts to flow out into stories. I hope you enjoy them.

Aileen Toce, 2022

❧❧❧

Rocking with coffee in hand this morning, I drifted back to past times in my thoughts. Scarlett O'Hara told Ashely Wilkes not to look back, for it would tear your heart out. Perhaps she was right. Best not to look back to what might have been, but instead forward to that which is yet to come. You can wait so long for something to happen that you miss the gift of the present. The past has long left us taking with it the now that we let slip away. We are told that the future is not ours to know, and it certainly is not guaranteed to anyone. Time and tide wait for no man....or woman. I now regard time much differently than when I was younger. I find I now have a new appreciation of it. Though I try not to waste time. I do not 'idle' well. This trait stems directly from my mother. If you were just sittin' around, she would find something for you to get busy doing. To her, idle hands were the devil's instruments.

Lately though, I find I sit a bit longer on the porch swing with my coffee, throw the stick a bit longer for my dog, and in general, take in things around me more thoughtfully. After a certain age, time morphs from slow summers that never seem to end to speed racer on steroids.

A light snow fell again last night. My woods look like someone has sprinkled them with confectioners sugar. As no one is here to shame my laziness, I believe I'll pour another cup of coffee and watch the snow melt.

Sundays have a special feel to them. No one comes here to do any work, and a sign on the gate at my property's edge says, "No Visitors On Sunday, Please". Even close friends have learned to leave me be on Sunday. Being Catholic allows for Mass to be attended on Saturday, and shopping for the week was done on Friday. The peacefulness of the day seeps into you like worms in chestnut wood. I read till my eyes ache, work at an ongoing puzzle, and most Sundays, perk a second pot of coffee. I can wear sweatpants all day as not a soul will see me. Makeup can be dispensed with as there will be no one for me to frighten without it. I absolutely refuse to dust a single thing, will not pull out the vacuum, and eat only that which requires no cooking or causes me to wash any pots and pans.

What difference, you might ask, is Sunday versus any other day of the week to an older retired person? If you don't feel it, I can't hardly explain it, but Sunday is different. I don't jump up in a hurry to accomplish anything on Sundays. I have even managed to smother my usual Catholic guilt in the face of such extreme laziness. Sundays are for restoring the spirit, relaxing the body and refreshing the mind. A little R and R and R, if you will.

On Sundays, I feel a bit like a Union worker, and my retirement labor laws allow me to refuse to do window washing, scour anything, nor labor at anything more strenuous than feeding my dog. Let's face it…even the Lord, after six days of creating, felt Sundays were special, and He sat down and rested. I can totally relate.

❧❧❧

In the darkness this morning, I lay remembering my grandparents' farm. Sleeping in a feather rope bed made of dark walnut with a headboard so high that I'm sure the house must have been built to accommodate it. Grandma's biscuits as big as Granddaddy's hands - so fluffy like biting into a mouthful of cloud. That country life required that many chores get done every day. Chickens to feed, cows to milk, fields to plow, and canning to be done. There was a purpose to all that the farm asked from its people. And, in return, it gave back. Food from its fields, water from its ground and contentment from the very air you breathed. And the quiet. Something I don't think city people appreciate or even understand. I've been to the city. You can't hear your thoughts the same in all that hustle, bustle and noise.

Laying there half asleep, I pondered the gradual disappearance of country living. If you've never stumbled down a hill to use an outhouse facility in the coming darkness of evening, you just haven't lived! And during that trek being alert to a yard rooster convinced he was a watchdog. One that would bounce on your back with the stealth, accuracy and injurious intent of a ninja warrior. Then no, you haven't lived a country life.

If you haven't had corn pone from a cast iron skillet slathered in home churned butter set next to a bowl of speckled butter beans cooked in fat back with chopped onions....you've been missing out. If you haven't gone to an old two-story log barn before dawn in the cold of a fall morning to harness up a team of Belgian horses, watching a cloud of fog leave your mouth with every breath...you've been cheated of a real pleasure. The nuzzling of horse noses, their big lips searching your finders for a treat, the smell of oiled harness leather and hay filling your senses.

If you haven't drawn water from a well behind the house, you haven't really tasted water…water so cold it numbed your throat going down, and so good you'd drink more than actual thirst called for. If you haven't lived in a holler so peaceful and quiet you can almost hear crickets rub their back legs together and watched deer so at ease they nibble grass all round your house, then you can't really understand the peacefulness country living ingrains in the soul.

City folk come, but don't really get this. They bring noise with them. They disturb and disrupt peace at every turn. Perhaps in time they'll get it. Like the aging of fine wine, in time they'll come to absorb and feel country living. Hmmmmmm, but then maybe not.

⚜⚜⚜

Through the years, I have met many people. Being the sort of person I am, I tend to take people in. I take them to heart, as my mother would say. I can't seem to keep people at arm's length. Perhaps in today's world, that would be safer, but it wouldn't be my nature.

I have been blessed with some very dear, very old friends. I call those my thick and thin friends. The ones you call on to laugh with you in the good times and know you can call on in tough times. Friends are one of God's best gifts. Since He can't be everywhere all the time, He invented friends. When your spirit is low, they lift you up. When you find yourself wallowing in self pity, they give you a needed kick in the rear. They tell you the truths you may not want to hear, but need to be said. They revel in your accomplishments and feel the pain of your life blunders.

In recent years, I have begun to lose some of my oldest friends. Their passing, a reminder that time is short. A reminder to hold your friends that are left a bit closer.

Some of my friends have been with me for many years. I guess they now qualify as 'old' friends. Older than dirt, as one of my girlfriends says. She's the one I take shopping with me. She is that friend who will tell you how awful you look in something. One of my oldest friends is my "dead body in the back yard" friend. She's the friend you call when you've put down your sick dog or your cheating husband. She comes immediately to help with shovel in hand, no questions asked, no explanations necessary.

Friends take up different places in your heart. Each loved equally for different reasons. Each filling a need they met when we gravitated to them in the first place. One friend I talk books with…my reading buddy. Another, like myself, does needlework. One is an avid gardener. I could talk plants with her for hours. One is a follower of NPR radio, and he relates to me the best stories. I value our long talks. Those talks one can only have with the dearest, closest of friends.

Friends are like pearl beads on the necklace of our lives. Each bead a reminder of a friend and how much each one means to us. Each bead a cherished memory.

Having recently moved to a new town, I am starting over making new friends. One by one, I'm finding them. New beads being added to my necklace. They are not 'old' friends yet, but in time, in time, just maybe if there's enough time….

⚜⚜⚜

Blowing in the winds of recent conversations, slipping nonchalantly from tongues lately I hear the word 'war'. It starts that way. I recall it sidling its way into our collective consciousness then blatantly waltzing constantly off our tongues during the Vietnam War. It morphed from that to a barrage of news commentary, hideous television images and politicians lauding the courage of our young men and their dedication to the fight for freedom. Most of those politicians who never served and wouldn't know the butt of a rifle from the barrel end. During the Civil War, families waited at the local courthouse for the casualty lists. Vietnam brought a knock to your front door. A knock that forever changed so many families.

I hear the clanging of the war machine in Washington. Oh, it will be a small noise at first. Gradually, when the sound becomes common to the general public, it will startle us with its deafening roar as it rolls over our weak protests. We are slowly acclimatized to the end result we vaguely, if at all, see coming. We are slipped a few statements regarding 'boots on the ground', a mention here and there about some 'military shipments' and a news whisper about 'military support'. Soon the juggernaut of war rolls over us all disguised by slogans of democracy and freedom.

Perhaps it wouldn't hurt to listen to the words of songs from our past...Barry McGuire's 'Eve of Destruction', Buffy Sainte-Marie's 'Universal Soldier', Pete Seeger's 'Where Have All the Flowers Gone', and the one that is as relevant today as it was years ago, Bobby Darin singing a song written by Tim Hardin called 'Simple Song of Freedom'. Hear these songs, really listen to the lyrics. Remember that we've been duped by political rhetoric in the past. Let us be mindful of what comes after the politician's slippery speeches meant to draw us in. They aren't as rousing when the flag draped coffins start coming home. Pay attention…the winds of war are blowing.

When the world was thought to be flat, at the edge of the known world, the old map makers wrote, "Beyond this point there be dragons". It indicated to sailors that venturing beyond the known territory, they would sail into an abyss and disappear.

How much easier might our lives have been if we'd had warnings of the 'dragons' ahead? Life offers no road map. We stumble along, reaching a fork in the road, and as Yogi Berra said, "Take it"... we do.. often taking the right fork when the left one might have led us to a different life path. Life rolls on, and we with it.

Time moves on and eventually allows us the vantage point of looking back on our journey. Hindsight, which is always 20/20, allows us to see clearly those turns in the road not taken, that might have offered a better way to go. Since life doesn't offer a 'do-over', we must be satisfied with the route we chose.

All journeys reach their end. So, too, our trip will run its course, that final destination will be reached, and we will stand before the great 'map maker'. We must remember to tell Him of our gratitude for the journey, and that even the 'dragons' along the way made the trip wonderful!

It's hard to learn something you don't think you need to know. We humans are stubborn creatures. Even in the face of blatant fact, we will still cling to our mistaken judgment on an issue. Acceptance of being wrong can be a hard pill to swallow. My daddy always said that it took a big person to admit when they were in the wrong. Usually we are not sorry for our actions, but terribly sorry we got caught.

I imagine that the greatest percentage of confessions on wrongdoing are brought about by religious guilt weighing on our conscience. For Catholics, the weight of guilt can sit as big as a millstone around your neck. In sixth grade during a test, I overheard a child next to me whisper a test answer to a classmate. It was an answer I needed, and I used the whispered knowledge to correct my test question. That Catholic millstone got heavier with each passing hour that day, and before noon had me back in the classroom confessing my shame to my teacher. I wouldn't reveal who had whispered the answer, just that I'd used it on my paper. Though she praised my honesty, I still got an 'F'. The worst was yet to come. I knew I had to tell my daddy. After I had relayed to him my woeful tale of character failing, he asked me what I had learned from it all. I told him that I felt like a thief cause I'd stolen the answer. In his wisdom, he said I wasn't a thief so much as I'd made a poor decision not doing what I knew was the right thing to do. The consequence of my actions and the 'F' had me grounded from any fun activity at school and mucking out the horse stall for the next month.

As I lay no claim to wearing a halo, I admit that my moral compass has tilted on its axis a time or two through the years. Always at those times I have felt the weight of the millstone and had my daddy's words echo in my head louder than Quasimodo ringing the bells of Notre Dame. Age has helped me learn to swallow the pill easier and admit when I'm wrong, and to exercise better judgment, most of the time, in the first place. Should my moral compass point me in the wrong direction, my dad's words and that Catholic millstone are always there waiting to help adjust my course.

⚜⚜⚜

Christmas draws near. The tree is up. Lights twinkle, and ornaments sparkle. Boxes filled with delights are tied with satin red ribbons. The house is shrouded in a blanket of ermine white snow. Smoke twirls up a chimney rising from a roaring fire beneath. Clad in jammies with a Santa face on the front, a little girl sips hot cocoa sleepily watching the tree lights. It was that rarified moment in time between belief in Santa and questioning. That blissful bubble of innocence when all things are still possible.

A horse was my Christmas request….every year. Now at seventy, I look back and recall those memories. Christmas still delights my soul. The colors, the lights and the sense of joy it brings. I seem to smell evergreen trees and cinnamon candles everywhere I go. Turning on the outside lights in early December, I feel almost giddy.

The years fall away; I am that little girl once more. Only now, the joy of Christmas is more in the giving and less about the receiving. More about the peace and less about the bustle. The season brings out in everyone a generosity of spirit and a kindness of heart undimmed by winter's chill.

Christmas heralds the end of another year. A closing of a chapter. This season's memories will be added to our fond recollections. It has been said that memories are the garden of the mind from which we harvest solace in old age. I now understand this to be true. I do not know what the pretty box under my tree holds for me, but I am certain it is not a horse!

There were several things my father would not tolerate…a back-sassing child, not keeping your word, or a scaredy-cat daughter. He worked diligently to insure I did not grow up with a fearful nature.

When it was time to learn to swim, he tied a rope around my waist and tossed me off the dock. He pulled me along the length of the dock. I'd go under, and he'd pull me up, telling me to use my arms and kick my feet. In short order, I learned to swim.

Before I was ten, he put me in a hunting blind with a rifle, a jug of water, a blanket, a roll of toilet paper and a bucket for "the necessaries". He told me he'd be back in the morning, and if anything came over the platform edge, be it man or beast, to shoot it. It was years later when I learned that he'd stayed all night very close by in the woods. His lesson was that I should learn self -reliance and not to fear the darkness nor being alone.

He taught me to shoot, to handle a horse, to stand my ground when I was right, to care for those less strong and to keep a promise. He wasn't a man to mince words nor to waste them on idle conversation. So great was my desire to make him proud, I'd have walked five miles on broken glass if he'd asked me to.

There is much written about the maternal bond, and I understand that as I am a mother; but more credit ought to be given to the attributes a father can impart to his child….strength of faith, character, and loyalty. Like those taught to a skinny little girl with freckles.

Seconds after the clock ticks past midnight, we are assured that the old year is gone. Revelers blowing tiny cardboard horns herald a new year as confetti covers Times Square. I always expect to feel something at this time of year that I don't. It has nothing to do with my age. I didn't feel it at twenty either. Just another day drawing to a close with the usual expectation of the next day dawning. I do, however, at the close of a year feel the weight of Catholic guilt.

Jewish folks tend to feel they have the corner on the market of GUILT. I, personally, beg to differ. As a Catholic I know I can carry guilt with the best of them. No doubt about it. Why, I can even feel guilt for someone else's sin. How, you might ask, does guilt fit in with a new year beginning? Well, here it is....looking back on the passing year, I am pressed by all the hoopla to ponder whether or not I have squandered those twelve months. I can feel the quivery, bony finger of guilt tapping on my shoulder. Have I made someone's life better? Have I eased the burden of a friend by word or deed? Have I enriched the world around me by being in it? Have I done anything in that year that I should be blessed with being granted the next one? I hope so, but guilt sits nagging in my ear that I could have done more, been better or tried harder.

As hope springs eternal in a cockeyed, albeit Catholic, optimist like myself, I know in my heart that a new year brings another chance. An opportunity to do that which I'd left undone, right my wrongs and appreciate my shortcomings as they, too, give me a chance to be a better person.

My good intentions beat down the bony finger of guilt, and I feel quite smug that I've done so. Then I remember eating a handful of nuts I'm not supposed to eat, and sure enough....he's back. Happy New Year!

⚜⚜⚜

Poor judgment has a multitude of euphemisms. Like being so blinded you couldn't see it coming. Or being a person so trusting that you 'missed the signs'. We tend to rationalize poor decisions to forgive ourselves for being foolish. Often we continue along the same path just to avoid the confrontation change inevitably brings.

Holding one's tongue often causes less conflict than speaking one's mind. Where, though, does a person draw the line in the sand as to when to put up or shut up? All decisions come at a price. With hard decisions, the bar is set a bit higher. Some decisions are like crossing the Rubicon….there's no going back.

Procrastinating on resolving a problem is living in limbo, but deciding on a course of action does have a consolation. There's a peace that comes when you've set a new course. A contentment that knowing a matter has resolution. Feeling that sweet spot of internal confidence, knowing you're on the right track.

My grandmother always said that there was never anything in life so bad you couldn't "pick yourself up, dust yourself off and start again". Words to live by, words to live by….

⚜⚜⚜

Isn't it funny how life turns on a dime and has you going in a direction you weren't expecting? Seems about the only thing in life you can 'set in stone' is your name on your headstone. All else seems a roll of the dice. We've all heard the old adage, "We plan, God laughs". That seems a bit cruel. I'd rather imagine that He doesn't laugh so much as He sits back waiting to see how we handle the curve ball we've been tossed.

Life is a gamble. You play out the hand you are dealt. The cards come across the table, you pick them up to see what you've got to work with....a great hand or one not so good. Life is like that. You deal the best you can with the hand you've been dealt.

Health issues, family tragedy, financial ups and downs, heartbreaks....all of it comes with the game called life. I had a plan, my cards looked good....four of a kind at least, and then....the dime dropped. I was suddenly holding new cards.

I don't know if God sanctioned it, changing circumstances allowed it, or if I just followed my heart, but my course altered, and I finally came home to these mountains.

When your cards get reshuffled, you never know what you'll get. But in this game called 'life', isn't that all the fun? It isn't dull or boring, and you never know....your next cards might be a royal flush!

My momma always said that giving from your plenty didn't please God near as much as giving when you had little. If you needed it and yet shared with others, God smiled and would bless you in double measure. My momma lived by those words. She often gave when it hurt to do so.

My parents married during the hard times of the Great Depression. Finding work was not easy. When my daddy was hired on with a short run trucking company, it meant a bit more food on the table. He was paid $7.00 a week - big plenty in those days. Every day, twice a day, in good weather and bad, he walked three miles each way in the early darkness of morning and the same each evening.

One year, they decided to give both of their boys a new bicycle. They chose the bicycles at a local store and put them in layaway. Every Friday, my daddy made a small payment on the bikes. To help out, my momma took in ironing and sewed for folks. After months of small payments, the bikes were paid and Christmas was nigh.

My daddy took the boys into the woods to cut and drag home a small Christmas tree. They made popcorn garland, stars from aluminum foil, and an angel tree topper from a toilet paper roll, bits of ribbon, scraps of fabric and cotton balls. The stage was set. Santa was coming. The boys' excitement was contagious. Their enthusiasm made the tiny rented house glow.

On Christmas Eve, my parents walked to town. They would each push a bike home. Daddy was to later recall that he was so worried the wind would separate them that he tied a piece of rope from his belt to my momma. She was barely 5'2" tall and uncommonly tiny. It was a long trek home. Their clothes and shoes were no match for the bone chilling cold and snow. That night, my momma had frostbitten feet. My daddy rubbed her feet and did all he knew to do for her. Still she lost all her toenails.

Christmas morning at first light, two little boys rose to find shiny new bikes beside the tree, unaware of the price paid for their joy. Years later Daddy said it was months before the boys stopped grinning. He and Momma both said it was their best Christmas ever.

It wasn't about the ramshackle house they lived in, the meager food on the table, the small tree with no store-bought ornaments nor the trudging miles through the cold and snow. It was the simple pleasure of bringing happiness to their children. My parents' Christmas joy was found in the spirit of true giving....literally giving till it hurt.

I was raised in a loving home, fathered by an extraordinary man of extreme good looks and uncommon character. He called my mother his "Queen in calico". Mother read voraciously. Her quilts won ribbons at the fair, and her fly fishing ability was legendary. They told me the sky was the limit and to reach for the stars.

I was educated, married and lived a city life. A long, long way from my 'raisin'. Secretly, in my heart of hearts, the little voice that speaks to each of us in quiet moments never stopped whispering to me that I didn't really belong.

I was raised with people who spoke of the seasons and planted by the Farmer's Almanac. Men who talked of killing hogs when the moon was in the right 'sign'. Women I'd grown up around talked of canning, pickling, quilting and knew to soak your foot in a tub of kerosene if you stepped on a rusty nail.

Every parent wants their child to do better in life than they had. To leave the nest and to soar high in the world. But what if our roots never let us go. What if those roots cling to us like the tentacles of an octopus, ever encircling, grasping and pulling us back.

Perhaps contentment in the soul comes to each of us in being happy where our heart feels grounded. There is magic to be found in the pleasures of an ordinary life lived amongst good folk who share the bounty of their gardens, the kindness in their hearts and the church pew with their neighbors. I finally listened, that little voice telling me to go home is stilled.....I have come home to roost.

Far be it for me to imply that I have any profound knowledge on any given subject, but I do know a little something on the topic of washing machines. I guess I should know a bit about them, as I'm convinced that at birth, girl babies get an invisible stamp on their foreheads that says, "does dishes and laundry". As I've tried in every relationship I've been in to get around it, I guess my forehead stamp stuck because I am invariably the laundry and dish doer. But, I digress…let me get back to my washing machine.

Mine has a habit of stopping, just for a moment, at the beginning of the wash cycle just as I turn to walk away, and, of course, that makes me turn back and pause a moment. I'm beginning to wonder if my machine might have a sick sense of humor! Might even delight in seeing me shake my head as I walk away. Then there's the sock matter. I firmly believe my grandmother's wringer washing machine never 'ate' any of her socks. Mine does. I don't know where they go, but disappear, they do. Never in pairs, only single socks. Presently I have three pairs of socks with no mates. I know without a doubt that they went into the machine with their sock partner. It's almost enough to send a sane person over the laundry room edge.

Not to be beaten by a sadistic washing machine, henceforth, when I close the lid and hit the 'on' button, I will no longer look back as I walk away with a noticeable smirk fixed on my face; and I'm going to wash my socks in a zippered laundry bag! Ah, sweet revenge. Grandma said that getting revenge was like grabbing a snake….it'll turn round and bite you. Perhaps I'd better keep a closer eye on my mischief making machine!

❦ ❦ ❦

Lately I have begun to grasp the full meaning of "in the blink of an eye". It's about life slipping away. Like sands through an hourglass, the years are escaping my grasp. As though a black caped magician has waived his wand and thirty years were instantly whisked away. It seems only yesterday I was young, thin and my hair hung almost to my knees in waves so thick two hands couldn't hold it. Where did that girl go? The years alter each of us, and hair turns grey.

Life happens, opportunities present themselves, doors open, and we walk through them. Our lives being driven by one thing or led by another. Youthful decisions that weave their way down through the years, altering our futures in ways we could not foresee. Choosing paths, not knowing where they might lead. It is said that time and tide wait for no man….or woman. A course is chosen, and years go by following it.

I could not have known back then that a child's love of a place could settle so deeply in my bones as to etch a permanent desire in me to return. It nestled deep inside of me. Hidden quietly away, revealed to no one.

Life's plan took me far away, but the longing in my bones to go home became so painful as to refuse to be ignored. The urge to return burned in my mind like the beacon from a lighthouse guiding ships on the sea. I had no choice but to capitulate. The yearning in my heart was so great I felt compelled beyond all reason to follow where it led. I can not agree with Thomas Wolfe, for I know beyond a shadow of doubt that you can go home again….as I am here.

Loving someone lets them in. The veil is raised and the curtain dropped on your innermost feelings....your heart as vulnerable as a child's, and your emotions exposed. As nothing else can, love allows another's barb to strike your soft underbelly....to wound without mercy. Love destroys the cloak of protection that previously encircled your heart just as surely as the horns toppled the walls of Jericho. Like water seeping into a crack in a retaining wall, slowly widening the tiny crack until the wall gives way and love flows in.

There's almost no stopping the fire once love's spark is ignited in the heart. For better or worse, the heart just gets us in too deep to back out. Like Sherman marching through Georgia, our resolve is trampled with little hope of ever rising again to be in control. Just as the outgoing tide sweeps shells back into the sea, love's tidal wave engulfs us in its depths. We, like the shells, are powerless to fight against it.

Personally, I found relinquishing control over my heart so difficult that I couldn't let go. The dizzying roller coaster ride of emotions I saw my friends take in the name of love did not appeal to me. The ride always seemed to end badly, and I held at bay any attempt to offer me a ticket.

But when the right circus comes to town, you find yourself scrambling to get your ticket. The roller coaster ceases to be scary, and its ups and downs just part of the wonderful ride. Sometimes you have to just let go, throw your hands in the air and hope your ticket to ride lasts a lifetime.

❧❧❧

I recently moved to Sparta, North Carolina. The plan was to stay in an apartment there until I could close on my house in Glade Valley just south of town. Moving to a new place is always a daunting experience, doubly so when you know absolutely no one. Growing older I notice that I am no longer fond of driving at night….I am a danger to myself and others. I began my journey in daylight from Richmond, Virginia expecting to arrive in Sparta in the five hours Google maps assured me that it would take. As I am severely directionally handicapped, ten hours later, lost deep in the mountains in darkness, I realized I had taken a wrong turn as I found myself to be in Tennessee!

By the time I finally reached Sparta, I was unglued, unnerved and unhappy. Adding to my misery, neither my IPad nor cell phone's AT&T service was working. I could neither call for help nor ask directions from my realtor. Having anticipated my arrival many hours earlier in the day, he had long since closed his office and gone home, taking with him the key to the apartment I intended to sleep in that night.

Arriving in Sparta around 8:30 pm with my stomach growling, my composure shot and being more than on the verge of tears, I pulled into the Walgreens parking lot hoping to find a phone. A large truck was parked there and I could see someone on a cell phone. Knocking on the truck door I asked a young man for help, telling him my tale of woe, explaining that my realtor's office was closed and asking him to make a call for me. As I rummaged through my purse hunting for the number he asked my realtor's name. "Greg Miller", I replied. Before I finished his name the young man said, "He's my cousin" and was dialing the number.

My grandma said that God knows every sparrow that falls to the ground. That night I was the sparrow....overwrought and exhausted. I felt alone. I'd arrived where I knew no one and yet had connected with my realtor's cousin. What are the odds of that happening? I'll tell you....none. God doesn't do odds. He's always a sure bet.

Driving in the pitch blackness of the mountain roads, I asked God to watch over me. Had I disappeared into a ravine, no one would have even known where to begin searching for me so far was I off my intended travel route. God had done that, but it didn't occur to me that He'd go so far as to deliver me right to the person most able to help me. Oh, me of little faith.

I spent that night at the Alleghany Inn, still exhausted, but no longer feeling alone or lost. Like the sparrow I was guided by the hand of the One who always knows the way home.

More than canoeing, skiing, hiking, antiquing, or bird watching, western North Carolina has one other valuable unheralded attribute… peacefulness. If it could be bottled like spring water, they'd be selling it too. It's that super fine thing you can't get in a store. You can't buy it, barter for it or steal it. To gain it requires you to stop racing through life, to slow down and drink in what's around you. Acquisition of more things won't garner it, trading up to a bigger house won't give it to you, and it can not be gifted to you. Amazon and Walmart do not offer it for sale.

My dad always said that all things of value come at a price and to be careful about what I was willing to part with to get them. A lifetime has passed since I first heard those words. Reflecting on his words, the weight of them sits heavy on my mind….what choices I made due to misjudged value and at what cost? Fortunately, with a new day comes new opportunities to make better choices.

Peace in your soul is like that other valuable commodity, time. It's precious and not to be squandered lightly. You know when that peacefulness takes hold of you. It's a religious experience without guilt, a natural high without the drugs. If you don't have it, get it. Stop what you're doing and find it. Grab it with both hands and don't let go. Throw over the traces of whatever stands between you and internal peace. Light a fire in your belly to feel it. This life is not a dress rehearsal for the next act. This is IT, and time is short!

Coming home to the quiet of these mountains came at a high price for me, but Daddy was right….peace in one's soul is so valuable, no price is too great to pay for it.

⚜⚜⚜

Recently, a flock of turkeys made their way across the field in front of my yard. As I watched them hop, amble and waddle their way round the tall grasses stopping to nibble at some unseen bug or seed, they made delightful little noises. It occurred to me that with Thanksgiving so near, they might all be earmarked for a platter. Such peculiar, not very attractive birds. I find it quite humorous that Ben Franklin wanted to have the turkey as our national bird. Imagine that beak on our coins!

Coffee in hand, I sat watching the flock. They did not pester one another, did not squabble over a juicy bug, nor did they jostle for lead position as they wandered about. One turkey appeared to be older. He was more gray than the others, and carried himself with, dare I say it, a quiet dignity. Of the whole group, he alone kept an occasional eye on me. I thought him a wise old bird.

Watching them, it occurred to me we might take a page from their play book. They were so peaceful going about their day. They weren't rushing to be somewhere else, weren't concerned with their appearance, had not the slightest desire for 'more' of anything, and were apparently living in harmony with one another. They were living in the moment, content with their place in the 'big' picture and appeared to have no fear of the future.

Like flowers in the fields, the turkeys neither toil nor spin, yet take their place in the grand scheme of life. Finishing my coffee as they moved further from my sight, I thought how being a turkey isn't such a bad thing after all.

My grandma had a button collection that she kept in an old tin box. I loved to fill my hands with the buttons and let them slide through my fingers back into the box as a miser might with gold coins. There were buttons of every shape and size in a rainbow of glorious colors. Years later, inheriting the button box, I discovered that it contained some unusual buttons. There were many Bakelite buttons, a couple Civil War era buttons, many mother of pearl ones, and a few made from horn.

Grandma taught me a lot through the buttons. Knowing my enjoyment of them, she used them to help me learn math, a subject I found very difficult, to say the least. She made a game of sorting the buttons and counting. Teaching me my "sums" as she called it. A child learning small lessons through her invented game. Buttons were soon to teach me a more valuable lesson.

Going uptown to the fabric shop with Grandma was a big treat. A wall of shelves stacked with bolt after bolt of fabrics in more colors than my Crayola crayon box. Passing my hands over nubby dotted swiss to the exquisitely soft velvets was pure Nirvana. There were spinning racks filled with hundreds of beautiful buttons and wooden stair stepped risers with spools of thread lined up like tiny soldiers in colorful parade dress uniforms. As Grandma talked with the owner of the shop, I wandered around dreamily in this world of color and texture.

Our trips to town were what Grandma called our "girls day out". Our trips always ended at the local diner for a soda pop and a "sittin spell" as Grandma was usually tired from our walking. As we sat waiting for our sodas, I pulled a red button from my pocket. I'd found it at the fabric shop on the floor and pocketed it. As I turned it over in my hands, I looked up to find Grandma's piercing dark eyes watching me. She inquired as to where I'd gotten the button. I told her. She then asked if I had paid for it. "No ma'am", I answered. Grandma was about to teach me a lesson. One others might have felt unnecessary to teach, but one I have never forgotten.

As our sodas arrived at our table, Grandma explained that taking anything you didn't pay for was stealing and worse yet, it was a sin. I may not have grasped the concept of theft, but I knew full well how Grandma felt about sin. She did not waffle about sin. It was black and white.....period.

With our sodas finished and Grandma rested, she marched me back to the fabric shop. There I apologized and paid for the single button. Though the shop owner wanted to dismiss it, Grandma insisted I pay for taking what was not mine. Then Grandma ushered me to the button rack and allowed me to pick two cards of buttons. She handed me the money to pay for them, explaining that these were to start my own button collection. I was elated. I'd returned to the shop feeling ashamed of myself, yet left feeling Grandma's kindness in the lesson.

Grandma wasn't done. Arriving home, I was sent outside to rake and bag the fallen leaves from under her giant magnolia tree. I had to feel the cost of the sin of stealing and the payment for the red button I'd taken. It wasn't the amount of money paid, it was the price of building character.

To this day, I cannot pass a fabric shop without going in. I still collect buttons, and I am grateful to Grandma's lessons that made me a better person.

How do we know when the love in our life is a great love? The love we were meant to find. That person that completes us. If only there were a magic way to see love's truth before you gave your heart away. Like poker players at a felt-covered table watching the next card fall with a placid face, but…is there a 'tell'? That little thing that tells the other players what cards are truly in your hand.

Does real love have a 'tell'? Is a kiss that curls your toes the sign? Is being weak in the knees the 'tell'? If your heart pounds so hard in your chest you think it might burst….is that the big clue?

All those are physical responses. Although exciting, not necessarily a good way to make a partner judgment call. Maybe a deeper assessment is needed. Does this person sit comfortably in church beside you? Does kindness to animals and little children come easily? Which takes priority to this person, giving or receiving?

My grandmother said if a woman couldn't cook speckled butter beans in bacon fat and good cornbread, that a man should look elsewhere. Might not be so applicable in today's world. My mother felt that if your husband had to be to work at 7:00 am, then you rose at 6:00, cooked him a good breakfast and sent him off with a smile and a prepared lunch. She did just that. They were married 58 years.

Maybe love's 'tell' isn't something you can see in the early stages of romance. Perhaps it shows itself to you years down the road after that person has stood by you through thick and thin. When he puts your needs ahead of his wants.

Maybe he listens and acts interested even when you've talked ad nauseam about your feelings. Or he brings wilted wild

34

flowers he picked earlier in the day because he knew you'd like them.

Perhaps it's in the loyalty and trust built on years of being together. Knowing he knows you almost better than you know yourself. When your back is against the wall, you know he will stand beside you for support and in front of you for protection.

Perhaps in the end you can only hope the card you've been dealt is a good one. An Ace of a partner who makes your life a winning hand. And later as you put those wilted, roadside Black Eyed Susans in a mason jar of water you'll know....he's definitely 'the one'.

In my front yard stands a massive cherry tree. Being nearly as old as Methuselah, it has weathered a great many storms, suffered through many a bone chilling winter and been a nesting site to hundreds of birds over the years. Under its huge arms my yard is shaded, and I find respite from the hot summer sun as I garden. Currently every branch and twig is covered in little buds eagerly waiting to bloom. Soon the entire tree will be ablaze in cotton candy pink. Such beauty fairly takes one's breath away and makes you want to give thanks.

God's altar isn't always at the front of a church. Age has gnarled its limbs, broken off some in violent mountain winds, and large root knots grip the earth, straining to support so large a canopy. Watching it accept its advanced years, changing with ease through each season, I feel I might learn a lesson or two from my old tree....to accept that which I can not alter and learn to bow gracefully with what troubles life may send me.

In due course, my lovely tree and I will have something in common...for I, too, will be as old as Methuselah!

❧❧❧

In the fireplace, gas logs send up flames to warm this tiny cabin. The world outside has become a wonderland shrouded in drifts of cloud-like whiteness. As predicted, snow fell all night and will continue all day today. I am housebound and love it.

As darkness begins to fall, I will light all my kerosene lamps and enjoy the glow they give. Before electricity came to these woods, I'm sure many families used them as their only source of light. Oh, I'm not longing to go backwards in time. I don't miss my grandfather's outhouse, drawing buckets of water from the well, cooking on a temperamental wood stove and straining to read by the oil lamp. But I do hanker for the spirit of those days.

Of course, I'm remembering them through the rose colored glasses of a child's perspective. Grandma's biscuits the size of a man's palm, water from the well so cold it took your breath away, everyone around the fireplace talking, oil lamps flickering shadows on the walls, Grandma reading from the 'Good Book', making notes in the margins, and floor boards that creaked with every footfall. But truth be told, I would go back if it were possible.

Back to a time when everything moved at a slower pace, children actually played outside, when men shook hands to seal a deal, and helping your neighbor was common. Yes, I long for the smells emanating from Grandma's kitchen with pots of speckled butter beans simmering in bacon fat and onions eaten with cornbread slathered in butter…and no doctor constantly nagging me to watch my cholesterol levels. I'd surely die sooner, but what a way to go!

'Crossing the Rubicon' means there's no going back. How many times in our lives have we drawn a line in the sand? Taken a stance that can't be withdrawn? Put down a foot to make clear our point and found ourselves as stuck in cement as Jimmy Hoffa? I have done so once or twice with devastating consequences.

Feeling a sense of moral superiority or just plain stubbornness, I felt justified in my actions. Through the lens of age and distance, I occasionally question those prior set-in-stone decisions. But then, hindsight is always 20/20, isn't it? It's easy to look back and find fault with an old decision, but not as easy to see clearly your path while mired down in the difficulties of the moment. Perhaps second guessing oneself is just human nature.

Unfortunately, life does not offer us a crystal ball, a Ouija board, nor even an eight ball with a few easy answers to solve our problems. My grandma would have said, "You do the best you can with what God gave you. If life knocks you down, you get up and keep going". She had plenty of experience at both, so I take her words as gospel.

Looking back changes nothing, and only tears at your heart. Everything isn't always black and white....there's some grey area in most issues. Going forward, I'll try to draw less hard lines, look closer at the grey area and, unlike Julius Caesar, not cross the Rubicon if I can help it.

38

Little girls and their daddies have a special bond. My daddy was, of course, the strongest, bravest and most handsome man in the world. He was in fact a dead ringer for Clark Gable, but I didn't know that then. He adored me and I him. If I wanted something, he found a way to get it for me. Though his spoiling came backed up by a strong dose of discipline.

He was my rock. His very presence comforted me, gave me strength. Each Christmas, I was allowed to ask for something special that I really wanted. This particular Christmas, I knew exactly what I wanted....to stay up late enough to actually see Santa arrive at our house. I'm sure they did their best to dissuade me from my resolute request, but I wouldn't be deterred. Nope, not even doll bribery could change my mind.

Years later I was to learn the real antics that went on that night as my dad tried to fulfill my heart's desire. He and our neighbor, Bob, concocted a plan to bring Santa to our home. The sleigh drawn by Bob's Belgian Draft horse wasn't hard to line up, the Santa suit was part borrowed and part sewn by my mother. They even spray painted an old pair of his work boots black. The red velvet toy-filled bag was made by my aunt from leftover fabric from a school project. Bright, wrapping paper covered empty boxes to fill the bag my dad was to sling over his shoulder.

To make me believe that Santa was on the roof, our neighbor was to make noises of walking boots. The scene was set. The tree glistened with colored lights, shiny ornaments and silver hanging tinsel. I recall being giddy with excitement....I was really going to see Santa. While other children were rushed off to bed for the magic entrance of the jolly man bearing wondrous gifts, I alone was going to see him.

My dad said animals in the barn needed checking and left the house. I stood on the sofa, watching out the living room window holding my breath and straining to hear the first sounds of sleigh bells. Then I heard them….faintly tingling in the distance, then louder as they drew closer. The winter moon threw golden shadows across the snow covered drive.

Soon the sleigh pulled slowly into view with 'Santa' (my dad) holding the reins and doing his best "Ho Ho Ho Merry Christmas to All" routine. My mother recalled later that she was certain I was holding my breath the entire time, and my eyes were as large as saucers. I watched as 'Santa' stepped from his sleigh and climbed a ladder to our roof. I guess I found Santa climbing a ladder credible. The sounds of boots on the roof was my mother's cue to hustle me off to bed. She told me that if I wasn't truly in bed, Santa wouldn't come down the chimney; instead, he would move on to another house. I remember fairly flying off the sofa, leaping into bed, and squeezing my eyes shut so hard it fairly hurt.

The part of the story I didn't know until years later was to become the best part….apparently, my dad had considered almost all aspects of the 'Santa sighting' operation except the slipperiness of a tin roof covered in snow. Still holding the velvet bag, my dad began sliding off the roof. Bob grabbed to hold Dad, and just as quickly was himself sliding right behind him. Daddy's 6'4" frame landed feet first into the deep cushioning snow piled high around the house, and Bob landed right beside him head first. They helped each other dig out, and they rode the sleigh pulled by the big Belgian to Bob's barn. Mother said had I not been fast asleep, I'd have heard two grown men laughing loud and heartily at a stunt gone awry.

She always thought the "cheer" in the Christmas eggnog may have had more to do with slipping off the roof than the sliding snow! Daddy had come through that Christmas night as he would continue to do through the years for his little girl. He was the steadfast rock I could always lean on, count on, rely on. Many Christmasses have passed since that one, but none hold such a special place in my heart. For who among us can top seeing 'Santa'?

Recently, an unhappy friend told me that she needed to get away. I pondered her statement and concluded that happiness isn't something you can run away to find. It isn't a Disney World trip. Contentment isn't bottled and sold at the Belks perfume counter.

Through the years, a number of my friends have married and divorced in the futile search for someone to make them happy. Though not personally being the fount of all wisdom, it does seem to me that happiness comes from within. It's inside each of us, just waiting. I would not want to be the sole, all encompassing source of another's happiness. Goodness, what a burden that would be indeed.

Perhaps a contented spirit comes with getting older. Wisdom and good judgment are said to be attributes attained with age. Having reached the 'age' part, I still occasionally shock myself at my apparent lack of either. So perhaps not always or in every instance does true wisdom and good judgment surface. Unlike cream rising to the top, it just doesn't quite get there. But happiness….that one I've got down pat.

To find it, I have but to walk these woods enveloped in the cathedral-like silence among pines larger than columns on any church. The body relaxes, the mind settles and the spirit soars. Happiness and contentment ooze from every pore of my being. I know why my daddy hunted and my mother loved to fish. It wasn't the kill or the catch nearly as much as the peace they felt in the woods or on the lake.

Finding happiness is a personal journey. Not something provided for you by someone else, sought out by a change of scenery or won through the lottery of birth, social status or wealth. It's there in each of us just waiting for us to set it free.

⚜⚜⚜

Recently, I found myself working diligently and with great fervor to support, or so I thought, someone I cared about with some problems. I'd seen the path needed to reach a good resolution for these issues, and put my own priorities on the back burner so as to devote myself to the more pressing, important issues of my friend.

As my friend is not good with paperwork, follow through and necessary contact phone calling and appointment scheduling, I took the reins, put the bit between my teeth and proceeded to whip the issues into shape, setting up a game plan for proceeding towards the ultimate goal of finding a solution to everything.

Somewhere along the way, I missed the signal from my friend that he was more than happy to not repair what was wrong, to ignore the overwhelming evidence to the contrary indicating help was necessary and to blithely bury the issues under a misdirection of the facts better than a slick magician.

There is little in life that does not teach us a lesson. Albeit not always a comforting lesson, but nonetheless, provides us with a nugget of wisdom. It rang in my head as loudly as Quasimodo ringing the bells of Notre Dame....You can lead a horse to water, but you can't make him drink!

❦ ❦ ❦

Growing up, there wasn't a telephone in my home until I was in high school. When one was finally installed, every call was a long distance charge so it was seldom used. A CB radio allowed us to communicate with my father's pickup truck and my brother's home nearby. We lived so far from town that I rose each day at 5:00 am to catch the bus to school. My mother shopped for 'store bought' groceries about every six weeks.

I recall being surprised to learn that most people purchased meat for their dinner tables from a store. Prior to that revelation, I assumed everyone ate what their father hunted or grew in his garden. In an assembly line process, the bass fish my mother caught were breaded then layered between waxed paper, bagged and frozen. Five huge chest freezers meant a bounty of food was always at the ready for the constant flow of company welcomed at our home on the lake. It was nothing to have twenty friends staying on a weekend.

By comparison, I now live a Trappist monk's existence. Laundry was twice a week chore, and we hung clothes to dry on a line. A dryer was considered unnecessary, and my mother died never having owned one.

I had a horse, a dog, a cat and books that transported me to worlds far away. I was an 'armchair traveler' long before I understood the expression. When my daily chores were done, I spent long hours roaming the woods on my horse, coming home only when darkness was closing in. I carried a sandwich, a bottle of water and my father's pistol in the saddle bags. All highly unacceptable, I imagine, for a ten year old girl in today's world.

Most of the childhood I enjoyed has sadly gone the way of the buggy whip. Today a cell phone seems a child's right of passage from the crib. Kindle is today's library, and nearly lost is the joy of turning each page of a book so good you just can't put it down. The freedom to roam unchaperoned and unharmed has also been lost in these times.

Back then, my life held no fears. We wore no masks for fear of breathing in germs, and hearing our National Anthem brought tears to our eyes and a hand over our heart. Thomas Wolfe told us that we couldn't go home again. But, were it possible, I'd be packing my time traveler's bag in a heartbeat!

Judas Iscariot sold out Jesus for thirty pieces of silver. "Thirty pieces of silver" has become synonymous with betrayal of any type. I see such betrayal here in these glorious mountains. All around me, stunning tracts of timbered land are being ravaged for someone to get their thirty pieces of silver. It takes years for the stripped land to recover. The monies gained from raping the land is long gone before the trees, shrubs and grasses ever return. The natural beauty and habitat that is lost to the logging companies can not be measured in dollars and cents. I am not fool enough to not understand the need for money, but stripping land bare for thirty pieces of silver is tantamount to selling our collective soul. It is on an equal par with Judas's betrayal of Jesus....and we all know how badly that ended for him!

⚜⚜⚜

Sometimes we all have troubles in our lives. You might say you've been dealt a bad hand. Best to lay those cards down and step back from the table for a bit. When the cards are reshuffled and a new hand dealt, you may find you have more aces than you know what to do with. You can't fold and go under just because of a few bad cards. You have to play the cards you are dealt, win, lose or draw, just stay in the game.

Only until the last card is dealt and picked up can you really know how the game will go. Stay in till the end, count your losses and wins, and know that life offers a tomorrow full of new cards, a new game and always a few aces. We're all in a bad game once in a while. How dull would life be to win all the time? Some of the best outcomes in my life have come after what I considered a losing streak.

That's the fun of the game….not knowing what cards will come next. But you keep playing, you hang in there hoping for an ace or two. Personally, I'm gonna sit at the table as long as I can and hope my cards are good ones. When they aren't, I'll play out the hand I'm dealt as best as I can. I've been very lucky, and The Big Man dealing my cards has always come through with an ace just when I've needed it. Tomorrow brings a new day, a reshuffle of the cards and always the possibility of a long winning streak!

Each of us is raised with our family's set of 'shoulds'. Things we are taught to do or not do as dictated by our individual family code of conduct. Many 'shoulds' passed down through the generations. My grandmother had a whole plethora of 'shoulds'. "You 'shouldn't' say anything if you couldn't say something nice." "Children 'should' be seen and not heard." My father used to visibly cringe when relating one of his grandmother's 'shoulds'.

Arriving at church on Sunday all the children would pile from the back of the wagon to play, while the grown ups greeted one another. The womenfolk brought covered dishes for the dinner on the grounds meal and shared recipes as the menfolk gathered to swap hunting tales and talk of crop miseries.

As the preacher beckoned all to come for service, Daddy said that his grandmother would call the boys for a quick inspection before entering the church. Invariably, he was found wanting in appearance. She would spit on a corner of her hankie and scrubbing at his streaked face would say, "Lloyd, you 'shouldn't' go into the Lord's house looking like a heathen."

My dad grew up to keep some of those family 'shoulds'. He told me, "When you shake a man's hand you 'should' mean it, you 'shouldn't' ever speak ill of the dead or trust a man who grins all the time". My mother's most used 'should' was, "A person 'should' accomplish something every day. There are only so many hours granted to each life, use them wisely." Those were words to live by, from people who lived hard lives of honest work and simple pleasures. I best get up now as I 'should' do something constructive with the hours left in my afternoon.

✧✧✧✧

Spreading the last few bags of mulch in my yard yesterday, I was bathed in a shower of small yellow leaves. Not those of the major trees screaming their message that fall is nigh. No, this was a whisper, still I heard its message….fall is not far off in these mountains. Soon summer gardens will finish for the year, their bounty will be canned and a sweater will become a necessity.

I finished my mulching, made a cup of coffee and sat on my porch swing to admire my yard work. I'm not sure whether the coffee or thoughts of fall brought my grandmother to mind, but there she was. Fall was her favorite time of year. Rocking on her front porch with a hot cup of black coffee in hand, she shared memories of her past and lessons that serve me well even to this day. She always said that her coffee had to be as black as a Spanish lady's hair. Now, I doubt seriously that my grandmother had ever seen a Spanish lady's hair, but I knew what she meant. A spoon could stand in her cup of coffee and not fall over.

Grandma drank coffee pretty much non stop all day, every day. I guess she was drinking espresso coffee before it became popular. A pot of strong, put hair on your chest coffee was always perking in her kitchen. No matter the chores that had to be done, there was always time to have a cup and talk. Her hands were tortured with arthritis. Sometimes she laced her evening coffee with a tad of whiskey. She said it "soothed her bones and eased the pain".

Finishing my coffee I felt fall's nip in the air and pulled my sweater tighter around me. It's coming, I thought. We're on the downhill slide to Christmas. Like my grandma, I too have arthritis in my hands. Perhaps my bones would benefit from coffee laced with something other than milk! With a hot cup of coffee in hand, I plan to enjoy fall, ride out the winter and look forward to next spring….and more mulching.

Underestimating people, especially older folks, is common, but a mistake. Youngsters tend to marginalize us. Our appearance of frailty belies an inner strength that still lives within. There comes a time when one realizes that good looks have faded, that running anywhere is a silly thought, and our judgment is questioned even by ourselves.

I recall a time when men followed me around in Lowes, and now I'm so invisible I have to chase someone down for assistance. I have reached that age. It comes on slowly for most of us. The fading of what we were creeps over us like a glacier snow mass creeping across the Swiss Alps. Slowly but surely taking us over. The me that I remember has slipped away, and I live now with the me that I am.

There are benefits to this current version of myself....most times doors are held open for me, I get AARP discounts on purchases, when I forget appointments it's overlooked, and best of all, I don't have to exercise a filter on my opinions. It isn't always politically correct to call a spade a spade nowadays, but age gives one carte blanche to express truisms as we see them. Perhaps too much freedom. I bite my tongue frequently in an effort to curb that sense of entitlement. As long as I can still lift my 12 gauge to my shoulder if required, climb a ladder when needed and belt out the lyrics to any Led Zeppelin song that comes on the radio, then I'll consider myself still in the game. Putting my feet under my own table, paying my own bills for as long as I can and doing so with as much mental acuity and physical health as God allows me is the ultimate goal. I've made a list to put on the fridge to remind myself to count these blessings....if I could only remember where I put the list.....

It occurred to me that we writers of words allow the world to peek into our very souls. Writing lifts the magician's veil, exposing all secrets. Thoughts put to words lay bare the heart's emotions and the brain's hidden musings. Poe's dark side shocked us, Stephen King made fear palpable, Faulkner's south oozed from him in every word, and Harper Lee's empathy for those less fortunate poured from every page of <u>To Kill a Mockingbird</u>.

Words have such power. They can incite a movement, bring tears, break a heart or uplift a weakened soul. Words color our world, create images in our minds and titillate our imaginations. It seems to me that people are either 'word' or 'number' oriented. I can barely add, division makes me nauseous and fractions make me want to slit my wrists! But words, ah yes, the elixir of life. They pour unbidden from me.

Often during the night, I am awakened with an urgent need to write down thoughts. I even pull off the road to scribble down something I feel compelled to capture on paper. Be they quarter words you need a dictionary to decipher or penny words even my dog can grasp, words convey everything from our intentions to our longings.

We went from man grunting on the African savanna to a quill pen dipped in an inkwell, and words flourished. The ability to express oneself is tantamount to discovering fire, inventing the wheel and for those of us who write….more precious than all Silas Marner's hoarded gold.

⚜⚜⚜

Just this side of the grave, what will our last thoughts be? Will regrets of things undone or loving words left unsaid fill those last precious seconds? Will unmet expectations come to mind? Will a lost or unrequited love haunt the periphery of those final thoughts? Will resentment of old wounds hang heavy in our exit thoughts?

I can only speculate as no one has, as yet, returned to apprise me of how those last lucid moments went for them. My grandmother waited five hours expressly for me to arrive. She said that she wouldn't "go" until she had spoken to me. Sitting on the edge of the bed, I held her hand. Opening her eyes she spoke one final sentence. "Honey, God will bless you." With that, she drew her last breath and exited this veil of tears.

I don't know what my last thoughts will be or who I will hang on hoping to see one last time. But, like my grandmother, I hope my hand will be held by that one person who adores me, and I hope my thoughts will reflect the happiness I have found here in these mountains. Grandmother was so right....God has been kind....I have been very, very blessed.

My daddy had no grey areas. He did not waffle on anything. When he laughed, it was hearty and never at the expense of another's feelings. He was not boastful and never crude. Being a master carpenter, he built some beautiful things. As Jesus was also a carpenter, Daddy always said he was in good company. If he shook your hand on anything, it was a done deal. If he gave you his word, you could be the farm on it. When he started something he finished it. He was not a man of halfway measures. If he called you his friend, he stood by you. If he loved you, it knew no bounds. He had strong convictions and an even stronger personality. He was not prone to pointless anger, but if that genie came out of the bottle, you better find a bunker to hide in. He was a tall man with broad shoulders and in appearance was a Clark Gable copy. He hunted and fished to put food on the table. His animals adored him. I used to think he and his horse had an invisible connection so in tune were they.

Daddy always spoke to Jake, his redbone hunting dog, in a low tone. Jake watched his every move and obeyed his commands instantly. Their loving partnership was a delight to see. He was my hero. To say I adored him would be an understatement. My mother said that he had only one weakness....me. He was my staunchest supporter, my dearest friend and my protector. To have such a man for a parent was an honor and a privilege. In life's lottery of fathers, I held a winning ticket. He taught me courage when that wasn't necessarily a lesson for little girls. He showed me how to stand on my own two feet and to be accountable for my own mistakes. He taught me compassion and backbone and inner strength. Once a father like that is gone, you realize that never again will anyone ever have your back in quite the same way. There was never any doubt that he would have laid down his life for me. In good times, in bad, in danger, darkness or in sunshine, never again would there be such a knight in shining armor to come to my rescue.

The Coronavirus is sweeping across our land like Sherman marched through Georgia and with equal destruction. He laid waste to field and town just as this virus is leveling small businesses and toppling human victims. This unseen organism is as lethal as Sherman's sword. It brings cities and lives to a screeching halt. Whatever hopes and plans we had have been put on a back burner. We race down the road of life at breakneck speed until illness holds up the STOP sign. Really puts life in perspective, doesn't it?

Frankly, I've been rather enjoying this 'social distancing'. It is an enforced life break. As though a mighty hand hit the 'pause' button. I geared down my internal engine and am moving at a slower pace. This virus has a public relations campaign of fear. It makes health issues paramount in our thoughts and takes precedence over all. It stands out in our mind as a red bird might in a flock of crows.

The news media and our everyday conversations are of little else. I've decided to do the Ostrich thing....I've stopped watching the evening news, turned off the radio (yes, I still own one of those) and plan to do what those southerners did so long ago as they waited out Sherman's Yankee invasion. I'm going to hunker down, eat butter beans and cornbread crumbled in a glass of milk, help my neighbors when needed and hope the toilet paper holds out! Like Sherman, this virus will wear itself out, and we'll be stronger for having lived through it. Take hope, friends....the South will rise again!

⚜ ⚜ ⚜

A change is in the air. Standing in my yard, surrounded by woods I feel it....I hear it in the pines that sway to and fro in the wind like ballerinas in their own production of Swan Lake. That Granny Smith apple green color fills the woods now and fallen cherry blossoms cover the ground in a pink color like that of a little girl's tutu. The chill in the evening air has a less harsh feel to it.

A dogwood petal floats to the ground and settles next to my foot. It soon will fade. Each season leaves us with something to remember. Soon this one will give way to the warmth of summer. In the fields, corn will reach skyward, its silky tassels shining in the sun like spun threads of golden yellow. Summer will grace us with hot days, cool nights and watermelons so sweet you'd swear they'd been injected with Karo syrup.

My granddaddy judged how hot a summer day was by how far up under the house his hound dog went to get cool. If you couldn't see him, it was a hot day.

Folks say change is a good thing. I'm not so sure about that. I like things I can count on to be the same....the honesty of my friends, the love of my dog, the surety of God's word and the knowledge that one season leads into the next. Now that's something you can bet the farm on.

For now, I'm going to count on summer coming and not give too much thought past that. I plan to sit on the porch, swat a flies, watch bees bore holes in my rafters and think serious thoughts of splitting open a watermelon.

There is an invisible thread that runs from parents to their children. I speak now only of the mother/child connection because that is the one I know best, for I am a mother. A mother of an only child….a son. I had never intended to have children. They were not in my plan, especially not at 38 years old. I had a fantastic job doing international letters of credit for a bank and loved my life.

Things changed and I found myself in a hospital surgery being handed a baby. Talk about a new life path! He became my sole focus. Had the invisible tether been the anchor chain to an ocean liner, I could not have been more connected to him. He was bathed, pampered, powdered, cuddled and adored. Concerns over insurance for shipments overseas were replaced with worries over baby food quality and teething issues. The days and weeks of his progress turned into years.

I realized the tether that began at his birth was now as bound to me as a jungle vine wrapping around a tree. Each year settling deeper into the bark of the tree until they merge into one trunk. My little boy had become ingrained in my very soul and I his whole world. We were a mutual admiration society of two.

He went through the usual growth markers that all humans do. I aged, and he developed into a fine young man. Meeting "the one", his life took a new direction. He found his soul mate, and she became his focus, as it should be. I proudly watched as he progressed into this new life stage. The tether widened to include the lovely girl I thought would be a daughter. I was wrong.

There are many parents of estranged adult children. I'm sure we all share the same wounds and scars. The tether between my son and me was severed, and like the amputee with a missing arm, I, too, sense the missing part every day.

Death has a finality. The mourning lessens with the years. Estrangement is different. It lingers in the periphery of your very existence. It lurks just beyond the veil of your everyday life like a ghost in a haunted mansion. Turning suddenly, you catch a glimpse of it on a stair landing. Always on the edge of your consciousness.

Most days I stay too busy to be aware of my ghost, but I know it is there. Just waiting to appear in my mind when a quiet moment presents it with an opening to slip into my thoughts. I wonder if it is the same for other parents like myself? Are we, the cast aside, destined to forever live with only ghosts of the children we brought into this world and cherished?

It is a sad ending to a story that began with so much hope and love. It is said that memories are the garden of the mind from which we harvest solace in old age. If that is so, I will live with my ghost and be happy for his presence and the memories he brings. I am beginning to find comfort in his company.

Walking into Walgreens this week, I was reminded that February is Love's big month. Racks were filled with cards gushing romantic testimonials to it. Box after box shaped into big red hearts filled with candy were waiting to be purchased. Hallmark and florists wait eagerly to cash in on this celebration of romance. The sight of all those over-the-top expressions to love made me pause to consider the grip love has on our heart.

With invisible chains, it holds us prisoner. Love originates in the brain, but it is the heart that nurtures it, thrives on it and suffers because of it. Love can bring euphoric joy. It can also bring debilitating heartache. It brings us to our knees and causes common sense to fly out the proverbial window.

The fire of a great love can scorch a hole in our heart, leaving a gully-sized wound that never mends. Does the passion it ignites become a personal eternal flame? Will our emotional psyche be forever singed from its heat? Once encircled in its flames, are we as captive as a fly in a spider web? Does the beauty of it linger in our senses like the fragrance of a gardenia long after leaving a room full of them? Does it ever after color our life with its blinding brightness? Can the ghost of a great love haunt one for years? Does everything after it seem diminished by comparison? Does the ecstasy of a great love overshadow the pain of losing it?

Pondering all these thoughts on love left me certain of only one thing. If love knocks at the door to your heart, swing it open, grab love with both hands and hang on. Throw caution to the wind and let it take your breath away. For when the days grow long and the winds blow cold, you will be warmed by memories of the love that curled your toes and carried away your heart. Happy Valentine's Day!

❦ ❦ ❦

Someone asked me how I think up my 'stories'. I pondered on this awhile and came to this conclusion....when people talk to me or are around me, an unconscious process is happening. Their words are spawning fragments of ideas that come to me later. These things settle somewhere in my brain that festers as if I'd been pricked with a pin. Like a grain of sand inside an oyster shell, growing layer upon layer of nacre over the particle until a pearl is formed. My stories are the pearls in my head. Some percolate for years before exposing themselves to me. Perhaps like a good cup of coffee, they need to perk for a while.

Artists probably see colors in a different way than the rest of us. Bead crafters see a box of colored beads and in their mind's eye envision a lovely necklace. A potter spins beautiful dishes from something I only see as a blob of wet clay. Quilters see tiny printed cotton squares as inspiration for glorious designs. Musicians hear notes in everyday sounds that the rest of us pass off as white noise. An area of our brain is triggered by that which touches us. My trigger is words. They form ideas and from there to my hand scribbling down what my brain regurgitates is something I can not control. I keep a pad and pencil by my bedside because it even wakes me from a dead sleep. Words are stitching themselves together like a quilt...my unconscious mind shaping stories like the potter's wheel.

I've never thought of myself as a gifted person, but I do know that my stories are a gift. Beautiful release for a head filled with words, like a child's Easter basket after an egg hunt. The basket of my mind is filled with a jumble of colorful words that gather themselves into stories.

❦ ❦ ❦

The sandman skipped my house last night, and sleep eluded me. I wandered out to the front porch during the night, sat in one of the rockers and just listened to the night sounds. The darkness enveloped me in a shawl of cool stillness. No fireflies lit the blackness with their twinkling bodies, for unlike me, they were probably fast asleep. Rocking quietly, I heard and felt the presence of the little creatures. Leaves rustled, and there were occasional clicks and snaps here and there. Apparently, some others were awake too.

There in the darkness, I pondered my tomorrow. What I had to do, where I needed to go. Then as older people want to do, my mind traveled back. I don't recall looking back much in my twenties. Guess that's an exercise that begins later in life when you actually have something to look back on. It is said that memories are the garden of the mind from which we harvest solace in old age. I am fortunate that my life's recollections are mostly happy ones. My memories are like pearls stored in a felt bag. I can take them out one by one to remember them. This night they came with no rhyme, reason or particular order to my mind. Some in bits and pieces.

There, rocking alone in the darkness, I recalled my first corsage, my horse, Baby, and my dad. A ski trip to Colorado slipped into the mix of thoughts. Colorado has powdery snow so deep you could disappear into it. Snow so white, cotton paled in comparison. Air so rarified it stung on the inhale and equally so on the exhale. The only sound I heard was snow falling from tree limbs sagging under the heavy weight. Standing there alone at the top of the mountain, I remember feeling small in all that vastness. Hearing something larger than a cricket move in the woods surrounding me, I put away my memory trip. I replaced the memory beads in my imaginary felt bag, pulled tight the ribbon, saving them for another time when I will sit rocking in the darkness. For now, I'll leave the walk down memory lane and the creatures of the night, head back to bed and maybe, just maybe, sleep.

My earliest recollections of my father are mostly of trailing after him hunting in the woods, having to take two or three steps to his every stride. He was a tall man with legs that made a little girl have to hustle to keep up. He carried a shotgun across his arm. Though hunting with my adored father was a delight, I realize now that there was more in play than I understood then. As it was then and is now, it is being in the woods that feeds a need in me….something deep inside that is only sated by being in the quiet of the trees. There in the silence, my soul completely settles. Standing stock still, I feel the sway of the tall pines in a breeze. Each one pencil thin stretching skyward as if their limbs are offering an Alleluia to God. They mesmerize me with their dizzying motion so in harmony with one another.

Even knowing where you need to be, it can take a long time to get there. Life intervenes. It sucks up your soul in a minutiae of details, chores and habits that totally ignore what you really need. You keep steady so your children can flourish. Others' needs become your focus until a change happens. My life change was the equivalent of Tectonic plates shifting.

Never once during my seismic life eruption was there any doubt where I'd go. I'd always known these mountains of my people would call me home. They'd been calling for years. I heard their whispers, but I was too busy to listen. Finally, I have come home to roost. My little house nestles quietly in these woods I love so much. I am embraced in an ethereal welcome only a lost soul can feel.

I no longer have my dad to traipse after. He has been gone many years. I walk my woods by myself, but not always alone. I sometimes imagine his broad shoulders walking ahead of me, gun slung over his arm, reminding me to "keep up, Pudden".

⚜ ⚜ ⚜

Today while working in the garden, my mind wandered to thoughts of love. As I weeded and watered, I considered just how similar love and flowers really are. Without tender care and nourishment, they both perish. This vein of thought led me to ponder the heart.

The heart does not operate independently of the brain and the rest of the body, yet we refer to it as if it does. We refer to our heart as being lonely, willful or even giddy. We speak of losing our hearts to someone, of our hearts breaking, or of hearts yearning as though speaking of a separate entity.

Almost every family tree has one great love story in its past…a distant relative who went to their deaths in love with spouses that died years before. Or perhaps a spinster relative who never married after losing the love of their life in youth. Hearts damaged that could never mend. Country love songs remind us that not even death ends a truly great love.

Does the heart get imprinted with love? Does a great love in one's life leave its fingerprints on your heart? Is that imprint ever able to be written over? Once that love is felt, can the heart ever accept anything less? I think not. Once the heart has known the best, it can never fully accept second best.

The heart seems to allow us to compartmentalize love. In completely different ways, we love our parents, our children, our pets and our friends. The love for each powerful, true and intense in its own fashion, the heart making room for each.

Does the heart know time? Does it really break? Does it have a memory? Does it truly wither without love? I think yes. How does the heart know that special love that comes with certainty, perhaps only once in a lifetime? My heart always knew it was not satisfied. It waited in sleep mode. When that love came, my heart knew. There was no doubt. With no voice, my heart spoke to me: "He is the one."

Just as God in his wisdom allows the common rain lily to bloom in the garden next to the exquisite rose, He sends the beauty of love to pauper and king alike. Sometimes, if you are very lucky, He sends a special love that awakens the heart like no other ever has or will again.

⚜⚜⚜

A new year is a chance to begin a new game with an unopened deck. It's a bit like a high stakes poker game with God dealing stud. Some cards face down and some up. Only He knows the cards He holds for us and He isn't telling. He deals from the top, holds no cards up his sleeve and lets them fall as they may to each of us. Be you a high roller or just an occasional player, you play the hand you are dealt. Good cards or bad, joys or sorrows. In this game we ante up with our hopes and dreams.

I've been fortunate. I've been dealt mostly great cards. My game has had its share of high cards and aces, and occasionally a real losing hand. But my losing streaks have been mostly short. Overall, I'd say I've won more than I've lost. The Master Dealer has always given me the cards I required just when they were needed. I can say I've even had a Royal Flush a time or two.

As this new year begins, I'll sit in on the new game and ante up with my plans and wishes. As He slides the cards to me, I'll pick them up and fan them out. Just as all of us must do, I'll play the hand He deals me. A day will come when the cards are so bad I can't even bluff to stay in the game. All poker players know when it's time to fold and leave the table. It will be the same for me.

But for now…I'm in. A new year, a new game, and I can't wait to see my cards!

Recently, I passed a cemetery. An old cemetery. Unlike the perfect rows of newer cemeteries, this one had headstones that meandered in their alignment. Age had shifted the headstones, broken some, and others leaned cockeyed…listing to port…like drunken sailors stumbling back to their ships.

Turning my car to drive between the somewhat rusted iron gates, I parked and strolled among the headstones. I have always found cemeteries good places for quiet contemplation and introspection. I wandered, pausing here and there to read the inscriptions on the stones. Some so old they were difficult to read, some really sad, indicating the death of an infant, and one I'll never forget was the last word from an angry wife about an apparently philandering husband.

One thing they all had in common was that each had a story. Though I would not glean but a bit of it from those final words chiseled into granite slabs, I knew it was there…uncovered, unknown, unshared. Each lost story as silent as the grave the stones marked.

At one time, it was generally accepted that we would all come to rest in such a place. Now days you can be cremated and your canister of ashes carried into space. Some families even divide up a loved one's ashes. Folks used to carefully tend to family plots. Trimming the grass, pulling weeds and adding flowers to stone vases. Even in the movie, Gone With the Wind, funds were collected to spruce up the cemetery of the south's "glorious dead".

Eventually, old soldiers and old ladies like me join the multitudes of lost stories. I guess that's as it should be….ashes to ashes, dust to dust. My life story will fade from memory just as surely as those of the graves I wandered amongst. But I can tell you this: it is my wish to be deposited in a small mountain cemetery where I might rise up in the spring to see these mountains lush with new growth. In summer I will wander through fields covered with orange ditch lilies. In fall, my ghost will revel in the beauty of colored leaves on every hillside of my mountains. And in winter, I will bide with the earth watching each snowflake settle over me like a shroud of white ermine. There amid the trees, my story will be whispered by the wind, and perhaps a small part of me be remembered...

Snow was falling…silent and white. The chill in the house told him it had probably been coming down all night. Making his way down the hall, he turned the thermostat dial and listened as the furnace kicked on. Soon the house and his old bones would be warm. Since his wife died, his routine had been the same. Today would be no different. He'd get coffee on to perk and see if his paper had come. Going to the front window, he knew immediately that there would be no paper delivered today. It was also unlikely that his daughter would visit as the snow plows had not cleared his street.

Outside was a world of white as far as he could see. Parked cars were completely covered like cupcakes decorated in marshmallow fluff frosting. Smoke from his neighbor's chimney spiraled skyward. It was a scene straight from a Norman Rockwell Christmas card.

Christmas was just around the corner, heralding the passing of another year. Certainly a time of reflection for an old man living alone. Watching snowflakes fall, he remembered many a Christmas past. In that moment the pain of missing his wife was excruciating. Seldom was she ever far from his thoughts and especially so at Christmas. Sighing, he turned toward the kitchen to start his coffee and set out his mug. He would settle into his recliner and watch the early morning weather reports. An ordinary day in a life that found routine comforting.

That's when he heard it….a tiny whining sound. Had the furnace been running at that moment, he would not have heard it at all. Standing still he listened. The sound came once more from the back door. Frigid air hit his face as he swung open the door to find a tiny face looking up at him. A wee fur ball no bigger than the palm of John's hand lay shuddering on his back doorstep.

Thinking to himself that he certainly did not need this little bundle of trouble, he grabbed for a kitchen towel and bent down to scoop up the tiny, wet puppy. He vowed to himself and the puppy that as soon as the roads were clear, it would be taken to the nearest animal rescue. For now, he would find something to feed the little pup.

While heating some milk on the stove, he continued rubbing warmth into the puppy and discovered she was a girl. Cradling her in the crook of his arm, he dipped his finger in the milk and rubbed her mouth until she began to lick at his fingers for more. She was a sandy blonde and white color with brown, button-like eyes. Still carrying her, he rummaged through the refrigerator to find something soft for her to eat. Leftover mashed potatoes and a bit of gravy would be a start.

The little puppy viewed all this activity through half closed eyes. Sensing she was safe and warm, her nose began to take in the smell of food, and she lifted her head against the big man's arm. Setting her in his lap, he fed her tiny bits from his fingers. She swallowed hungrily. John wondered if he should put a sign in his front yard about the puppy. She had no collar. Just then, her small paw reached out to touch his arm as she licked a speck of potatoes from his thumb. After that small exertion, her head dropped, and she slept curled in his lap. Rest now, John thought, for tomorrow you're going. Pushing back in his recliner, both he and the little dog slept.

The day progressed, and John went about his usual habits with the addition of puppy care. Morning gave way to noon, and he made a sandwich for himself and a bit of something for the puppy. As needed, John took her outside to do her business and quickly back inside to be wrapped again in a fluffy towel he would heat up in the dryer. She seemed frail and weak to him, so he emptied a basket that held magazines, and as he moved about the house doing his chores, the basket moved with him. She quietly watched his every move with interest. Tiring a bit, John headed for his recliner. Lifting her to his lap, he chuckled to himself. Darn dog, he thought, but found himself scratching behind her ears. "Don't get too fond of this", he said to her.

His daughter phoned to check on him. They spoke of the weather, the snow and his ailments. He made no mention of the dog. As soon as he could drive, the pup would be gone. No need to mention her.

Day gave way to evening. He carried the puppy outside once more. The night sky was clear, stars twinkled in the blackness, and snowflakes fell silently on the blanket of white that was his backyard. Pushing a wing chair close to the side of the bed, he set the puppy in her basket on the seat. Corralling her he thought. John turned out the bedside lamp, admonishing her to go to sleep. Waking the next morning, he found brown eyes watching him, and a tiny tail making a thumping noise against the basket.

A new day came and with it, more snow. The snowplows had not come. John knew he would not be driving the puppy anywhere. His usual day began. But now a small shadow followed his every step. She was a Sheltie and was following her herding instincts, staying right on his heels. Fearing that he might step on her, John went to the garage in search of a box of Christmas decorations. He found a small bell and some ribbon and tied it round her neck.

The city and the old man hunkered down to ride out the fierce storm that lasted over a week. During that time, the lonely man bonded with the orphan puppy. He made a friend who accepted his gruff exterior, ended his loneliness and gave him a Christmas present he hadn't expected….companionship.

Finally, the storm passed. There was no trip to the dog pound, and a 'lost dog' sign was never put in the yard. John's life was changed. He now cooked just a bit more for his small friend, and he made room in his heart for the love that grew between them. The little dog brought so much happiness to his life that he named her Joy. Following his every step, the tinkling bell on her neck drove away sad thoughts and filled him with the Christmas spirit.

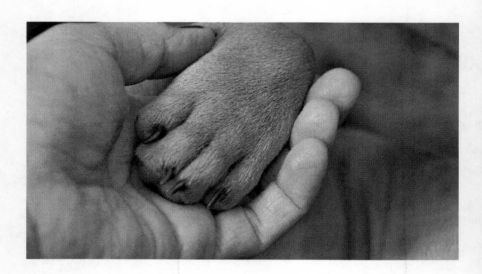

Recently at a party, someone said of my significant other, "He's a good guy.". Yes, I replied, a truly good guy. What constitutes a good guy? It caused me to consider things that I usually take for granted about him. All those little things that add up to a really good man. The things so embedded in his personality and nature that they go unheralded....an even temperament, a pleasant disposition, an encouraging outlook and a strong sense of loyalty. All combining to create an unusual man I really lucked into almost by accident. If the stars, the sun and the moon had not all aligned to place him in my path, we would not have gotten together. Perhaps that is really the case in most relationships. Are we not all just zipping through the space of our individual lives on a course that we have had little to no control over? Occasionally, two souls collide that are meant to find one another. That happenchance is what I consider the real 'luck' in the universe. Turning right when you should have gone left, staying when you should have gone, walking when you should have run or zigging when you should have zagged. I was in the right place at the right time and didn't realize it until much later. And yes, he is a really "good guy" and more importantly, he's my "good guy".

The days of our lives are measured by many things. We all progress through the familiar states of birth, childhood, adolescence and adulthood....all of us with similar triumphs and difficulties.

Our journey is measured through each year by the seasons. We plant our gardens in spring and vacation in summer. We drift from Halloween to Thanksgiving during fall in a blur of pumpkin carving and turkey roasting. Before we know it, the Christmas tree is being trimmed, heralding the end of another year. Our lives have 'seasons' to them as well. We graduate, most marry, begin families, some divorce, and all of us watch the progression of grey start to color our hair.

Society measures how well we have done by a measuring stick of our accomplishments and material possessions, how many degrees we earned, how large our bank account and how high did one rise on the corporate ladder.

Late in the game of life, after much trial and error, I chanced on the illusive and fabled 'soul mate'. Our time together is precious, and I find myself measuring it not to the standards of the world, but by my own yardstick. We particularly enjoy Sundays spent together. We watch the 'Sunday Morning' program, eat breakfast at a neighborhood diner and stroll through a local flea market. Afternoon usually finds us taking a nap, reading to one another from our favorite magazines before falling asleep. Lazy Sundays with easy pursuits. Simple days of hand holding, laughter and relishing our time spent in one another's company.

Many such Sundays have passed, and I hope for a thousand more. My days spent with him will be measured as contented and happy. What greater measure can be of a life than to have loved and been loved?

I have an old 1800's Gilbert wall clock. It is a large, elongated, mission style, dark wood clock. For its age, it keeps fairly good time. It has a distinctive rhythmic tick tock and chimes the hour and half-hour with the confidence of an elder statesman. Its age has given it an assurance that perhaps a newer, younger clock might not have.

If it could but talk, what stories it might have to tell of a life in service. Keeping many generations apprised of the time. It might tell tales of bouncing along in a covered wagon across vast open plains with settlers traveling across the country. Perhaps of rocking to and fro in the belly of a ship, sailing from Ireland with a family in search of a new life and more to eat than potatoes. Ah, if it could but speak, what tales it might share.

I have and have had many antique clocks....mantle, wall and grandfather. I'm as drawn to them as a child to a candy dish. They speak to me, and I want to take them all home. I have found clocks to be particular about where they are placed and can be as cantankerous as some people. If hung in a place that doesn't suit them, no amount of leveling will induce them to run. That may sound peculiar, but I found this to be the case with a grandfather clock I owned some years ago. Once running happily and keeping perfect time, I moved it to several different places I thought it would look nicer. After much effort and leveling in each place, it refused to run. Upon being returned to its original spot, it ran contentedly for many years.

Perhaps clocks like us find peace when we settle where we feel we are meant to be. Like sands falling through an hourglass, my clocks tick off the minutes of my days. They remind me that time is a precious thing that can not be recaptured once gone. My clocks also teach me that happiness comes from being content when you are settled where you are meant to be….for me it is the woods of these mountains that I love so much.

⚜ ⚜ ⚜

With Thanksgiving drawing closer, I pondered on the meaning of true thankfulness. We teach our children manners, right from wrong, to chew with their mouths closed, to respect their elders and in the south at least, to say 'yes ma'am' and 'no sir' if questioned about anything. But how, I wondered, do you teach thankfulness?

During the Great Depression, men stood in long lines, hoping to get a job of any kind, and in equally long lines for a bowl of free soup and a crust of bread. I'm sure they were thankful for either.

As an older expectant mother, I was urged to have amniocentesis to ascertain if my unborn baby was in any way handicapped. I refused and waited to deliver and love whatever I was given. He arrived perfect. I was thankful.

There are daily reasons to give thanks….my Katrina rose blooming again just as temperatures are beginning to drop, not breaking my neck as I stepped backward off a ladder missing the last step, a call that lets me know a friend's illness is in remission or a hot cup of coffee while I'm sitting on my porch swing watching hazy afternoon rays of sunshine color the field beyond my yard.

Thankfulness is not taught…it is felt down in your gut. Your heart swells with it. It fills my life not just at a turkey dinner in November. For years, I tried to return to this place I love. Finally I am here. I am truly thankful.

On this rainy, cold morning, I set to cleaning out my pantry. Tossing away this and that after checking the expiration dates. All that throwing out made me think of my grandmother. Waste not, want not…
that wasn't just a colloquial expression at my grandmother's house. Those were words you lived by. They ranked right up there with, "If you haven't got something nice to say, then don't say anything at all", or "If it isn't yours, don't touch it", and her favorite…. "Cleanliness is next to Godliness". As a child, I used to ponder on that one.

How, I wondered, did Grandma know for sure God thought being clean ranked right up there with being a good person? I didn't have to think on it too long, for if Grandma allowed it was true, then you could bet the farm on it.

My grandma lived through the Great Depression. Not a time recalled with fondness by anyone. It was hard. Hard like no one today knows about. Sure, we've had a toilet paper shortage at the grocery store, and that sent the local population into a tizzy. But the depression was Hard with a capital H. Like everyone, my grandparents were poor. They scratched a living from the dirt, made do with what they had and shared what they could with their neighbors. Everything was in short supply except their faith.

A supper on the table with nothing but collards, cornbread and rabbit was prayed over as though it were a feast. When a hog was killed, Grandma went to work. She used every single part of it. She made hogshead cheese, chitlins, and the feet were pickled.

Grandpa once said that if the pig's squeal had any food value, Grandma would have found a way to can it. Nothing on the farm was ever wasted. There was economy in everything they did. They weren't folks who rambled on talking. They said what they needed to say and always meant every word. Every morning they each got up knowing what chores needed doing individually and those they would need to work together to accomplish. No sleep aides were needed after the kind of day their farm chores required. A life of purpose that produced such hardy, good people.

Standing there, her words echoed in my head, "waste not, want not". Shame on me, I thought. I reached into the trash basket and pulled out that container of peanut butter and set it back on the pantry shelf. It wasn't quite at its expiration date. I felt sure Grandma was smiling down at me.

Unlike Ebenezer Scrooge's visitations from three ghosts representing Christmas past, present and future, my ghost is always the ghost of Christmas past. This time of year I begin to feel his presence. He lingers in the foggy periphery of my mind. Lurking in wait to take his place in the forefront of my thoughts.

Like Santa, my ghost carries a bag over his shoulder. He carries no gifts wrapped in brightly colored paper and tied with exquisite satin bows. What he brings me are flashes of memories of Christmases past with a giggling little boy. My ghost sprinkles these memories like Tinkerbell might spray stardust with her wand. These memories settle all round me in a torrent of thoughts that only another mother might relate to. From the first sign of Christmas, I feel the closeness of my ghost.

As winter approaches, a stop at Walmart is usually my first signal that he is soon to assail my mind with my locked away thoughts. All those artificial Christmas trees, snow-flocked ornaments and red tree skirts covered with dancing Santas trigger his appearance. Tables covered with pink, red and striped poinsettias for sale are the last straw…
my ghost emerges.

There's no holding him back now. I am inundated with a veritable flood of Christmas past memories that he sprinkles in my head.

My little boy laughing as the tree is raised, shaking boxes to guess their contents and cuddling next to me at bedtime as we read and re-read the traditional Christmas stories. These memories assault my heart, but there is no way to stop them. They consume me in waves of emotion normally kept under control.

No matter how grown they are or how far away they live, our children are forever ingrained in our thoughts, seared permanently in our hearts and forever our babies. A friend of mine, Jamie, refers to his teenagers as his "babies". I so understand that.

My ghost will shadow me all through the Christmas season. Christmas carols will open a mental door, and my ghost will zing me with those wonderful memories of an adored little boy in red jammies with reindeer on the feet.

Ghosts are not all frightening apparitions sent to portend evil. My ghost has become a welcome presence at Christmas. I've grown to look forward to the memories of now long gone Christmases that he causes me to remember. They come with no shiny wrapping and bows, but our memories are truly priceless, precious gifts.

An older, still dating friend called me to say that she was done with dating. After hearing some of her experiences, I'd be done too. When you are no longer the exotic bird you once were, it's difficult to preen and prance in the mating dance as we once did. Age clips our wings, dulls our feathers and has us flying a bit slower. But then, not everyone of us is fortunate enough to reach old age with a good partner.

My parents were married 58 years. I asked my mother once if she ever thought about divorce. "No", she said, "but murder, a lot". Many have sadly lost that soul mate partner. Seniors are now told they can search for a significant other on dating sites like Our Time and others. There was a time in the south that if your people didn't know his people, no connection was ever going to happen. What happened to meeting someone at church? Perhaps in this world of must-have nano second gratification, God just doesn't move fast enough.

Used to be that your friends had someone they wanted you to meet. Remember blind dates? They weren't all bad....well it helped if you were nearly blind! The water cooler at work let you get to know someone at your workplace. Do they still have water coolers? Probably not. Everything has changed or gone the way of the buggy whip....apparently old fashioned dating too. It's a brave new world now, and that includes seniors trying to find a companion.

Watching friends try to make their way in this new ball game, I am grateful I can watch from the sidelines and not have to still be in there pitching with them. So, if you find a good partner in later life, you better hold onto them like grim death as they are few and far between according to my friends still "out there" in the dating game.

I am one of the lucky ones. I have a significant other who loves me, finds my quirky ways cute and thinks I'm lovely too. The filter he sees me through may relate to some aging eyesight issues. When he gets a new eyeglass prescription, I hold my breath! We fly slower, and our feathers have dulled to gray, but we're still holding on.

Tonight, wind howls through the pines with the screaming sound of a freight train. A midnight train leaving from somewhere down in the holler, headed this way in the darkness. Cresting the hilltop, I hear it pick up steam, and the sound grows steadily louder. My windows rattle, and my little cabin creaks and groans under the onslaught.

All day, the winds have whistled and moaned their way through my woods and down the gulley and back again, oftentimes making a plaintive, eerie sound.

Trudging through the snow this afternoon, I made my way to the mailbox at the main road. Standing upright was difficult. Looking up at the tall pines swaying in unison, their movement almost made me dizzy. For these trees, this is just another winter season. Like any other in the past, and the same as it will be again in the future.

They bow gracefully under the weight of each snowfall and bend as the wind twists them near to breaking. These ancient trees, dealing with whatever hand nature deals them. A calm acceptance and a "just get on with it" spirit. Living in the moment....the season.

Perhaps we humans could benefit from learning to live with such an attitude. Living each day as it comes with enjoyment, allowing the natural order of things to guide us and accepting ourselves and others just as we are. Like the pines bowing gracefully in thanks for the good times and learning to bend with the difficulties.

⚜⚜⚜

I always wanted to be tall and svelte with legs so long a giraffe would be pea green with envy. As Dana Carvey would say, "not gonna happen". My female family members were all hiding under a stump when God was handing out legs to die for. He made up for short changing us in the gam department with other attributes....

My grandmother had a wit so sharp it could pierce metal. Aunt Mattie was such a good cook she could make soup from a stone. And then, there was my mother. Not only was she short...God threw in freckles and flaming red hair too. A trifecta of disaster for a girl not living in County Cork in Ireland. He obviously felt so bad that He overcompensated and gave her a veritable bushel basket of talents too numerous to mention.

One of the many things at which she excelled was fly fishing. Ah, it was a thing of real beauty to see her draw back a fly rod and lace the line in curving ribbons high in the air then drop the fly in exactly the right spot along the edge of the bank. She dearly loved to fish.

What I excel at, I've never been really sure. Perhaps we are bits and pieces of those traits that come down through the generations before us. For me, a bit of Grandmother's wit, some of my aunt's cooking talent, absolutely none of Mother's fishing skills and, sadly....short legs!

Life is a dance. Youthful days have one boogying into exhaustion. Mid-life has one dancing to a tune that others orchestrate. In this part of life, the dance moves very fast. Coming into these later years, I find myself dancing to a slower tune. I don't dip and twirl so much anymore. These days my dance is like the glide one feels dancing on a sawdust covered wood floor of an old dance hall.

I've heard the last call for last rounds; the lights are now low. My dance card has only one name on it, and his knees are no longer in any fit shape to trip the lights fantastic any more than mine. Though we do shuffle through the sawdust rather well together.

In movies, Ginger Rogers and Fred Astaire waltzed across marble ballroom floors so in tune with one another's movements, they seemed to move as one person.

For some, the same tune plays over and over for years. Dancing on with the same partner, moving awkwardly in steps terribly out of sync, unable to admit the need for a new partner or a change of music. We southern girls were raised to leave the dance with the one we came with, a sentiment not necessarily in tune with the reality of today.

After a long waltz in satins and silks, under crystal chandeliers that sparkled, casting rainbows of colors all round, I remember clearly the day the music died. My dance was over. Life moved on, and I began a new dance with different music and a new partner. After all these years, we are still in step with one another, two-stepping gracefully round the sawdust floor. The trick in life is finding the right partner to dance with.

❧❧❧

Weather reports say snow is coming. I eagerly watch and wait. Only a cocaine addict could be more thrilled than I to see several inches of white powder covering the ground. I even rise during the night to see if any has fallen.

In the white silence of these beautiful woods, my soul smiles. Contentment wraps my spirit in a warmth winter's cold cannot touch. Were I offered a chest full of gold, I could not be enticed to leave my mountain place. Though I have no bell tower, I am Quasimodo claiming sanctuary from my tiny cabin.

To say it has touched my heart would be an understatement. It has filled my senses with something not found everywhere ....peace and a sense of place.

All my life I knew I'd return here. It was inevitable. Coming here as a child to my grandparents' farm, I understood then as I do now that this was where I belonged. I spiraled through years of existing away from these mountains. They never stopped whispering to me to "come home".

Life intervened, and obligations delayed me, but I am here now to stay. I have answered the mountain siren's call. I am as rooted here as the tall pines and the strong oaks. As entrenched as the rocky earth underfoot.

No longer does my heart ache with an unspoken desire to go home....for I am truly home.

Flying from the University of Mississippi to an internship in New York the summer of his junior year, my son's career life began to take flight. This internship had the potential to set his feet on the journalism/photography career path he desired. It was one of those golden opportunities that don't come along often. I was reminded of nature programs that showed mother birds nudging their young from the nest, encouraging them to take their first flight. My little bird had never needed much nudging. From birth, he took to things not only good naturedly, but eagerly. As dizzying as it was for me, he was now jumping from the edge of the nest, and wasn't looking back. He was soaring up and away.

As a toddler, I recalled his first steps. After mastering the basics of actually standing for a bit, I watched as he stood looking from the chair he was holding to the sofa where he wanted to go. As always, I could see him considering his options. I could tell he was deciding whether or not to drop and crawl or to go for it and step into the open space with no hand or object to grasp along the way. After a moment, with a very determined look, he leaned forward and took his first real steps unaided. He beamed a toothless smile full of pride at me. With each of those steps, I wanted to take his hand and help him, but he needed to do them on his own, and I had to let him. He walked, and there was no going back.

When the first two-wheeled bicycle was purchased, I insisted on training wheels. I was certain they might prevent him from having too many scraped knees. I think they lasted about three days before he wanted them gone. He was a big boy and they weren't needed, he told me. I reluctantly took them off and watched as he wheeled away down the street. Again, he was moving forward, and I had to stay behind. He was pedaling on his way.

Getting his driver's license was a major growth point. A parent's nightmare come true. Would he learn the rules? Would he obey them? Would he use rational thought and good judgment behind the wheel? He watched, he listened, he read the book, and passed the test. With a lump in my throat and fear in my heart, I watched him leave the driveway for the first time. We said goodbye, and I waved. He drove away.

Packing up for college was the biggie. It wasn't summer camp - we'd had many of those separations. This was for long term and far away. With a packed up car and every protective bit of advice I could think of to give him, he was leaving again, and I had to stay behind. By that point, all training any parent can do should be done. The guidance, the admonishing, the words of wisdom, encouragement and praise - it's all been said. Then, just like now, I had to step back and watch him go. He left home.

They walk, they pedal, they drive, and if we are lucky, they soar - they really, really soar!

⚜⚜⚜

All day today, the sky looked pregnant with snow. It's difficult to describe to anyone unfamiliar with mountain weather. Fog hovers low in the hollers. Clouds seem heavy and feel close to you. The sky is a peculiar color.

Snow brings an unusual silence. The sky, shedding tears of snowflakes to give the earth a winter blanket. All the world around me goes quiet. Folks hunker down in homes with smoke from fireplaces spiraling skyward. Traffic on country roads is non-existent. Deer leave small prints across a grassy field now invisible. A strange peace envelopes everything.

There is absolutely no noise. Silence reigns, and every flutter of the birds at my feeders is made louder in the stillness. Tree limbs creak and snap under the weight of a night of snowfall. My garden bench all but disappears. Icicles hang from my roof like crystal ornaments left over from Christmas.

This respite from life beyond my mountain shall pass. Snow will melt, and the world will again intrude. For now, I drink far too much coffee, work puzzles, read and revel in the fact that I am joyfully snowbound at home. And, at least for a while, the busy world is locked out.

Sitting in a rocker before my front windows, I am as giddy as a child. I love snow, and the night has brought a magnificent bounty of it to my cabin. I realize that out there in the world beyond my little spit of land, snow is a burden. It slows traffic, delays deliveries, makes city streets a sloppy mess and in general, creates problems.

Ah, but here in my little corner of mountain heaven, it is a glory to behold. God's handiwork before my own eyes. Everything is shrouded in pristine white cotton candy fluff. It is as if a Currier and Ives print has come to life. Flakes are falling thick and constant and are the size of dimes.

I am mesmerized by the scene before me. All manner of birds fill their bellies from my feeders. They are happy to find such a banquet in the midst of a snow covered world. I find I can get nothing done but watch the beauty beyond my windows

Even Catholic guilt for being so lazy does not drive me from my window perch. For in a few days, the stunning beauty that I am privileged to see will be gone, and the laundry will still be there. I feel certain that even after the plagues of Egypt, some Egyptian woman still found a hamper of laundry waiting for her to wash. So I'll push the guilt aside and continue to sit here enthralled by the glorious scene beyond my porch.

Going to the VA Medical Center in Kernersville today with my significant partner of many years, I witnessed a touching moment that might ordinarily have gone unnoticed. Being in our usual hurry to leave, we were slowed down by an elderly couple walking in the middle of the carpeted path leading to the double glass exit doors. We slowed our pace as trying to rush around them would have been rude.

I took notice of them partly because their shuffling gait forced us to slow down so as not to collide with them. Then I noticed that they both had the most beautiful snow white hair I believe I'd ever seen. It was as though a cloud had settled on both their heads. But the real kicker that got to me came as they stopped walking. She reached up as he leaned down towards her, and she slipped his clip-on sun shades onto his glasses. So close to them were we that I overheard her say, "There now, it won't be so bright for you". After that, they began their slow advance towards the exit with us close behind them.

That simple act of loving kindness so grabbed my heart that I had to swallow hard and blink repeatedly to keep emotion from stripping me of my composure. My partner had not missed a beat talking, and the others rushing by had also not noticed what nearly overwhelmed me.

But isn't that what it's all about? This life quest to find another who completes us? Who loves you enough to look past your failings? Someone who puts your needs ahead of their own? That simple gesture of loving care made it clear for me.

In the end, when the good looks are gone, when health has diminished, when money no longer counts for much, the last priceless possession we really have is someone to love and be loved by.

At thirty-eight years old, I came home with a new baby boy. Having done only one babysitting job in my early teens, I found this a daunting prospect. That babysitting job had not gone well and only served to solidify my conviction that I was not a 'baby person'. This understanding of my own personality never waivered throughout the rest of my life. Against my better judgment, I was coerced into this present state of affairs and found myself staring into the blue eyes of a small midget. It was startling to see looking back at me a reflection of many of my own features and expressions. Having recently purchased a wok, I realized that I had come home with it bearing more instructions than I was given with this new baby. Talk about feeling inadequate! Popular opinion assures us that natural instincts would immediately take over. Hmmmm. By day two, I was waiting rather impatiently for any sign that those instincts were coming. Nature did take its course. In short order, I was overcome with the mother bear feelings for this little being that now depended on me for his every need. Healthy and strong he grew. He was born in September, and by that November, I had cause to give thanks.

In those early months, I diapered, bathed, fed, cuddled and carted him as though I'd had a dozen children before him. I gave over my life to him in a way I had not dreamed possible for myself. He became my sole focus and his every wish my command. His bath water had to be just the right temperature, his bottles prepared just so and his little clothes all bearing the 'Polo' label. I sang to him, talked to him, laughed with him and worried over him. While awake I showered him with love, and while sleeping, I watched him just to see his chest rise and fall with each breath. I was thankful as he progressed through each stage.

During the night, my eyes snapped open if he burped in his crib. No soldier on the front lines guarded his outpost as warily as I watched over my boy. I once heard that maternal instinct is stronger than that of self preservation. Later on in his childhood, I had a chance to prove that to be true. Coming to his defense, I felt adrenalin surging through my brain and was possessed by a blinding sense of protection that had no concern for my own safety. In that moment, I knew any danger to him would first have to come through me. It was my duty to him - no thanks were necessary.

Before he could properly hold up his own head, I realized that he would learn whatever I chose to teach him. This knowledge was a powerful obligation. Immediately I began a full scale determined effort to be the best teacher possible to him. He was fast and learned quickly. After all the basics, I began to focus on honesty, kindness and respect in ways he could see and absorb. I knew he was learning by watching as much as from listening to me. I delighted in his growth and praised all his successes. When he fell down, I taught him to get up. When he made a mess, I made him clean it up. When disappointments came, I told him even clouds had silver linings if you look hard enough. Even as a young child, I could see he'd taken my lessons to heart. He was a thoughtful, kind and loving child, yet he had spirit and backbone. I had done the best I could and was thankful of how he was turning out.

Time passed and he left the nest. He is now at college and soaring on his own. I am allowed glimpses of his new life in the phone calls he makes home. Pride swells in me for each advance he makes in life. In his retelling of the events of his week, I hear happiness in his life. I hope this inner joy came from something I taught him. He tells me of disappointments and the outcome of the situations. I'm hearing that he was knocked down, but got up. I know I gave him that. In another call, I hear of his sympathy for something that happened to a friend. In this I hear empathy for the problems of another. Another lesson he absorbed. He tells me of his work, and I hear pride in himself. I'm sure early praise gave him this confidence. For the man he is becoming, I am thankful.

Twenty-one Thanksgivings have come and gone since that first one with my boy. The small midget is now a man. He stands now on his own merits. He pulls now on his own boot straps to go forward in life. He has only himself to blame for his failings. I have given him all the lessons I could save one. That no matter how far he wanders or to what heights he soars, there is an invisible thread that connects us. A tether of love unlike any other in his life or mine. For this unique connection I am blessed and profoundly and eternally thankful.

⚜⚜⚜

Fall is a time for looking back. A year is soon to pass. It is slipping through our fingers as fast as the golden leaves of my cherry tree fall to the ground. Brisk winds are raining them down in such numbers that soon I'll be ankle deep in golden yellow drifts. Such a season reminds me of times that have passed, loved ones gone.

Great men throughout history have admonished us to be all that we can be. I wonder....have I done that? Have I even tried hard enough? When it is written down in the pages of The Big Book, will it be written, "She tried"? Will having tried count? Will having tried allow me a seat even in third class on the Bound For Glory train? When the dust of the years settles over my bones, will I or anything I have done be remembered by anyone? Most likely not. But then, good works and deeds are not meant to be tallied in public notice or praise. They are done because a need presented itself not in hope of a return of any kind.

Soon the last twelve months will be ticked off the calendar. Another year in my life gone, but with the hope of a new year looming I'll be given another chance to improve....myself, my deeds, my life. Perhaps, if I keep trying, I just might upgrade my ticket on The Glory Train to first class.

⚜⚜⚜

Christmas was once a race down the stairs behind a giggling little boy who couldn't wait to see what Santa had left under the tree for him. A live tree so large I needed a ladder to place every ornament, bauble and bow just perfectly in the branches.

Ah, that evergreen smell. Does it ever really leave your senses? Each year, trees for sale fill empty lots, and that smell permeates the air. The true fragrance of Christmas.

Poinsettias were my decorating theme every year. I filled the house inside and out with huge ones....only using the ones in that true Christmas red color. Even my gift wrapping paper was covered in red poinsettias. Adorning our homes and included in many religious ceremonies, the pretty plant from southern Mexico has become a standard of Christmas tradition.

Then life changes and we with it. Children grow up, move away, our lives become smaller and usually our houses too. Where once there was a Christmas Eve open house, a 10' tree, many boxes of ornaments and too many poinsettias to count, there is now a different Christmas. Just two of us....a smaller house, a tiny tree, a red poinsettia or two, and still lots of love to make our season bright.

❀ ❀ ❀

Of all God's handiwork, I find 'man' a real peculiar piece of work. We say one thing and do quite the opposite. There are things we see and those we refuse to see. There are secrets we keep and those we reveal. There are heartaches that are visible and others that stay buried deep. There are troubles we share and many we keep hidden. Some lies we tell ourselves and others used to deceive the world. There are lives lived in quiet desperation while others live desperately seeking quiet.

A facade of happiness can often disguise a heart full of sadness. We demand freedom in our words while in deed still deny it to some. We are beings capable of great works, unbelievable art and moving writings of feelings, wants and desires. It is said that this is what separates us from the animals. Yet the lilies and the creatures of the field neither "toil nor spin" and certainly do not worry. In their hearts they carry no jealousy, greed nor hate. The animals have no seven deadly sins. They do not calculate with malice to harm a fellow creature, and deception enters not their thoughts. Falseness and cheating are foreign to their natures.

Funny, isn't it that we human beings with all our faults, failings and often poor judgment have reached the top of the heap to lead the pack? We humans, for all the blessings granted to us and the "free will" we are allowed, still can not live in harmony. Perhaps those lower on the evolutionary ladder could teach us a great deal.

I'm about the only woman I know who would rather peruse a seed catalogue more than a fashion magazine, would prefer a day of yard work to a shopping spree and would highly value a truck filled with hydrangeas way over a velvet box with an expensive bauble inside. My father felt sure God worked His garden on the sabbath. When I asked my dad why he said, "Because hoeing the rows gives a man time to be thankful and pray". I guess God's house doesn't have to be four walls and stained glass windows.

Sun came to my cold weary woods today. Warmth filled my bones and brought on thoughts of digging in the earth. Two wonderful friends came by to help me clean out a flower bed. We chopped, trimmed and clipped. They generously help me accomplish what an aging back and arthritic hands won't let me do alone anymore. For them I am thankful.

Raking and cleaning up the garden bed, I understood what my father meant. The motion of the rake took over, the swaying pines whispered an alleluia on the breeze, a serenity settled over me and with not a pew in sight I felt prayerful.

Everywhere I look in my yard there are new growth buds. The cherry tree, the hydrangeas and even my roses all have emerging buds. A late frost or a freeze would be disastrous. I thought of consulting my Farmer's Almanac. Then I remembered….someone more 'in the know' than the local weatherman is signaling that a change is just around the corner. I'll put my money on Him and be looking closer at those seed catalogues, planning my order.

✤ ✤ ✤

The grey in my hair and arthritis in my hands belies a rock and roll heart. Those who read my newspaper column, pass me in the Food Lion or see me in the library would never guess a serious Led Zeppelin fan hides just beneath the quiet person they encounter. None would ever suspect that I sport a hidden Led Zeppelin tattoo.

Alone in my car, I indulge my passion for my favorite band....cranking up 'When the Levee Breaks' loudly and with lots of bass so I can feel John Bonham's drums thumping in my chest. Robert Plant belts out lyrics reaching a screaming crescendo that rattles the car windows and thrills my soul! How little we really know of our neighbors' secret selves.

The facade shown to the world often hides an untold story. In the town where I grew up lived a quiet woman. She had been a nurse during the Philippine Bataan Death March in 1942. She survived. Imagine the story she had to tell. There are people all around us who have lived, really lived! Lived lives of courage, excitement and variety. They are unnoticed because, sadly, there is an unspoken invisibility that comes with age.

So the next time you pass an elderly person going up the down aisle at the grocery store, perhaps you might be in the company of a retired marine biologist who sailed aboard the Calypso with Jaques Cousteau, a Peace Corps teacher who made a difference in distant lands or a nurse who was on duty at the hospital in Dallas the day President Kennedy was brought in. Most, like myself, with more to reveal than anyone would ever imagine. Rock on!

In the store, I passed a shelf offering egg dye coloring kits, yummy chocolate bunnies and neon yellow marshmallow peeps. It seems that no matter the true reason behind the season or holiday, consumer marketers have found a way to cash in on it. Now, don't get me wrong, I love biting the hollow ears off a chocolate bunny as well as anyone, but in the midst of it all, I try to remember the reason for this season.

For believers, we commemorate the day of the resurrection of a man who put into action what He preached. He suffered and died for us. No greater love hath a man that he would lay down his life for another. Those are powerful words.

As a child, I recall Easter as mothers quest for the perfect fabric with which to make my Easter dress. Only the search for the Holy Grail was fraught with as much dedication and fervor. It had to be the right shade of taffeta or the perfect pink Dotted Swiss.

I remember Easter as my mother fanning herself in the heat of the oak pews at church, of scampering over the yard in search of colored eggs and trying not to get chocolate from those bunny ears on my new dress.

It takes a good while for a child to grasp the real meaning of Easter. But when the meaning dawns, it is a moving revelation….a love so profound that even death was not too great a price to be paid. Though the dress is no longer a priority and there are no children to dye eggs for, I still bite the ears off a chocolate bunny first!

An old joke tells of men who during hunting season every year, went to the same place to camp. Along the way, they would stop at a general store for supplies and to talk with an elderly Indian man who could always be found sitting in a rocker on the store's veranda.

Every year they asked him how the weather would be during their hunting excursion. The old chief would give them his weather prediction. So accurate were his forecasts that the hunters began to rely on seeing him each year.

This particular year during their routine stop at the store, with their supplies purchased and loaded in the truck, they gathered round the chief and inquired of him how the weather would be for their stay on the mountain. The chief paused, scratched his chin and said, "Chief not know". Surprise and disbelief crossed the faces of the hunters circled around the old Indian. How, they questioned, was that possible?

Looking quietly at each man in turn, a tiny smile began to play at the corners of the chief's mouth and he said, "Chief not know cause radio broke". The chief had played the hunters for years, and laughing uproariously, he enjoyed the moment.

There's a parable in there for all of us. It is to look closely at that in which we put our faith. Before believing, totally sneak a peek behind the magician's curtain. Look deep into the jeweler's lens to tell if a thing that sparkles is really a diamond or glass. Whether we are choosing a partner or a president, remember to look beyond what shows on the surface. It's easy to be roped in by an image....like an old chief with a radio.

The Christmas I turned six, I got a Blue Willow China tea set. At eight, I rocked a pair of white street roller skates with pink pom poms on the laces. My tenth Christmas I got my first horse. At twelve, I got a custom made slalom water ski. By thirteen, Christmas presents began to be clothing oriented and continued in that vein for the teenage Christmases to come.

Years passed, and many a Christmas came and went. Adult presents were given, opened and most have been forgotten. The year I turned thirty-eight was to be my best Christmas ever. The present I received wasn't wrapped in shiny paper tied with an exquisite satin bow. It didn't come on a sleigh led by a reindeer with a red nose, and a jolly man with a white beard in a red suit did not shimmy down the chimney leaving my gift under the Christmas tree.

I didn't know it then, but it was to be the best present I would ever receive. For this present brought more joy than I'd ever dreamed possible and made a better person of me. It was a present I could not return. Nor did I want to.

There was no need for a gift name tag for I had no doubt it belonged to me, for you see, I'd spent nine months waiting to receive this gift. It was a six pound, seven ounce baby boy. The surprise was the red hair and Paul Newman blue eyes! He ranked number one above any gift I'd received before or since. It did not matter that he had a loving father and adoring grandparents in attendance....in my mind, he was all mine.

A gift that brightened my world with every toothless smile and made the spirit of the season more real to me than it had ever been. He epitomized the gift the original Christmas tried to teach us about.... unselfish, complete, never ending love. I named him Nicholas.

❀❀❀

Death comes to every door. No lock keeps it out, and no amount of prayer delays it. It's about the most sure thing in our lives. Because none of us are privy as to the date of our demise, no calendar marks the future impending momentous occasion. Hallmark has a card for everything, but I've not seen a card for 'death' itself.

We spend an inordinate amount of energy throughout our lives on celebrations for every conceivable happening … engagements, births, holidays, birthdays, weddings and showers. But not much thought is given to the big exit. In fact, most folks try real hard to ignore it. Truth be told, if we were sent a notice scheduling our impending passing, I suspect we might live differently in the time we had remaining.

As I sat watching the first snowfall of winter, a thought or two about death crossed my mind. Being past seventy, one would have to be brain dead to never give an occasional nod to the prospect of crossing the Great Divide. The snowy scene before me was so movingly beautiful that it made me sad to think that one day I would no longer see this stunning sight.

Then I recalled that I've asked for my ashes to be tossed out here in my woods. Even then in winter I'll see the brilliant red cardinals flitting from one snow covered branch to another. In spring wild roses I planted will send out new canes to climb over the old fallen down fence. Summer will follow, and wildflowers will shoot up where once there was a lane. And in fall, I will feel the earth changing as leaves turn from green to yellow to burnished gold and red.

I will be here, albeit in a different form, to follow life here in my part of these mountains. As to my time remaining, I plan to soak up every moment of life's beauty in this place I call home and give daily thanks for the Grace that brought me here.

Fall begins the race towards those seasonal holiday family gatherings. The ones we all wish could be like those Norman Rockwell paintings...mine were not. Uncle Bob Lee (namesake of the South's illustrious leader Robert E.) imbibes a bit too much while watching football, and his armchair coaching reaches epic loudness. Aunt Wilma's free spirit daughter arrives with orange and black striped hair, a spiked dog collar round her neck, rings everywhere on her body except her fingers and her sullen biker boyfriend in tow. Uncle Clyde's six year old twins, who have despised one another since birth, are at the children's table trying their best to stab one another with a fork.

Grandma, who isn't always certain who or where she is, has locked herself in her room to escape the chaos. The family cat, mindful that Uncle Bob Lee kicked him last Thanksgiving, is hiding behind the chest freezer in the laundry room. Daddy's red boned hound, Jake, lays under the aluminum table in the kitchen, hoping some scrap of anything will hit the floor. Both my father's elderly sisters are arguing that their green bean casserole is the best one on the table. My dad and his favorite grandchild are hiding out in the barn. Only dinner on the table will lure them to the house.

Cousin Dean, home on leave, waits patiently for a home cooked meal as he tries to make conversation with his orange haired cousin and the biker dude. Mamma looks frantic brushing stray, damp curls off her forehead. She's worried the mashed potatoes, cornbread, marshmallow sweet potato casserole and the turkey will never get on the table properly timed and hot.

Then, as it does every year, it all magically comes together. Food and family make it to the table. As Daddy begins grace, we hold hands to give thanks. Thanks that the twins aren't yet strong enough to mortally wound one another, that Grandma remembers who and where she is long enough to join us, that the soldier and the biker found space in which to tolerate one another and that as a family, albeit an unusual one, we come together to collectively give thanks. Seeing us all gathered round the table, I'm sure even Norman Rockwell would smile!

My much longed for winter has been slow coming this year. Most folks seem delighted that warm temperatures have hung on so deep into December. For myself, I constantly scan ahead on the ten day forecast models. I search for any hint that snow might even be a suggestion. I'll dance for joy at the first prediction of snow that puts those tiny snowflakes on the weather forecast charts.

Being retired allows me to happily anticipate that which working people dread. I'm like a school kid hoping for a snow day. There is a reason behind my desire for snow. You see, it slows down the world's pace. It brings to a halt all the running and gunning of modern daily life. Brings a near screeching halt traffic, and in that slow down, brings a quiet to our lives.

Standing on my porch holding a hot mug of coffee while viewing a sea of white powder is absolute bliss. The morning sun glistening on it, sparkling like candlelight bouncing off crystals on a chandelier. The only sounds heard are tree branches snapping under the weight of snow and birds chirping. My neighbor's wood burning stove sends grey smoke sprawling heavenward. In that quiet, thoughts settle and the soul stills.

Peacefulness covers the land, the mind and the spirit. The urgent need to go anywhere is removed, and we are forced to slow down. In the wider world, trouble may be churning, but here on our mountain, when the snow does come, it will bring a peace that is borne on each snowflake of that first snowfall.

We can not spend our lives wasting time on 'used to be', 'what if', or 'if only'. Today does not care about the past, and tomorrow will have its own issues. I'd like to think that I've learned something from my past, but maybe it's human nature that destines us to repeat the same old patterns again and again.

Thinking too much about yesterday only weighs down your heart and changes nothing. Scarlett O'Hara told Ashely Wilkes, "Don't look back, Ashley, don't look back. It'll drag at your heart until you can't do anything but look back". The fault in looking back is that the mind tends to shade things a different color than they actually were. The years falsify facts. Not intentionally, but because the details become fuzzy.

I had an aunt who was married for fifty years to the meanest, foulest man God ever let draw breath, but as soon as he died, a halo began to form around his deceased head. Soon thereafter, in her recollections of him, sainthood was bestowed upon his memory to the point I felt sure she might ask the church to canonize him!

Sometimes we give the past a glow it didn't really have. Like looking through rose-colored glasses, memories are altered to reflect the past as we would have liked it to have been, not as it truly was.

Perhaps some memories are best left cloudy like the fog that rolls over my mountain, shrouding all in a thick haze. The heart may rest easier altering the past with a little sugar frosting or leaving its truth hazy.

When Granddaddy sold a hog it meant a bit of money in the coffee tin on the shelf in the kitchen, but when he sold two hogs, they were in high cotton! Life was measured by how good the last growing season had been and wariness of what the next might bring. Would rains come too early or be too late? Planting was done by the Farmer's Almanac and a well worn copy of T.E. Black's, "God's Way Planting Guide".

Little in their lives was done without consulting the 'signs'. Teeth pulling, hog killing, crop planting and even hair cutting....all done during the right phase of the moon. They lived connected to the earth and close to God.

They took no more than they needed from the land and shared any excess with their neighbors. I never saw my granddaddy hurry, never saw him raise his hand to child or beast and never heard a profane word cross his lips. He was a quiet man, not much given to chatty conversation.

His barn was my favorite place. It smelled of hay, feed and smooth leather harness with an aged color that only years of use can produce. It was also the one place where I was certain that God resided. If I rose early enough to be standing inside the barn when the big double doors swung open as the first sun rays spilled in blinding me with golden light and warmth enough to chase away the early morning chill, I just knew God was there.

I'd sat in many a church pew, sang hymns in my off-key little voice and folded my hands in prayer, but I'd never felt God's presence as I did in Granddaddy's barn. It was a time that has passed, a way of life mostly gone now. It lives now only in my memory. Except when I stand in bright sunlight, close my eyes and feel His presence. Long ago, I began to realize He was everywhere with me, not just in Granddaddy's barn.

Funny thing about a really good friend....you often love them more than your crazy blood relatives, certainly hold them closer than your relatives through marriage and confide in them more than you ever would laying on a psychiatrist's couch. Besides, your relatives are inherited and your friends you choose.

A good friend knows your most intimate romance details, the personal failings you admit to and those you don't. When your dog is lost, your car won't start or you find yourself broke before payday, she's the call you make. If you've just buried a parent, she's the first knock at your door with comforting words and her best casserole dish. When your life's in a mess and better seems a long way off, she's there to lean on and to listen. She's the "dead body in the basement" friend with a shovel you can call whose only question is, "Where do I dig?"

They lift us up when we're down and give us a good shaking when it's needed. When all the world deserts you, a good friend joins your camp. Silence may be golden, but with a good friend, it's comfortable.

If you can say you have such a person in your life as a really good friend then consider yourself blessed, for we are not granted many such treasures. The older I get, the shorter my list of close friends becomes. Distance has parted me from some and death has robbed me of a few. Life does give us opportunities to make new old friends. I'm working on a couple of those now.

Thanksgiving....it's almost here. This year I'm going to cheat and go all out....I'm going to get the turkey that gets roasted in a bag, buy some instant mashed potatoes, open a can of green beans, make some quick stove top stuffing and plop a jar of jellied cranberries on a plastic plate....nah, not gonna happen.

My mother would roll over in her grave. Shame would be brought down on my head by all my deceased aunts. My grandmother would surely give me a talkin' to from the great beyond. Being raised a daddy's girl, the imagined disapproval I would fear most would be my father's. I just know that when I popped that bagged turkey in the roasting pan, I'd look up to find his spirit standing in my kitchen, arms folded across his chest, eyes glaring at me. Disapproval oozing from every pore of his ghostly apparition.

Though I am certainly not the best cook in North Carolina, I could make an effort to try and recreate the Norman Rockwell Thanksgiving image we all have in our minds. As there are only two of us to share the requisite feast, assembling it seems a daunting prospect.

Dare I ignore the possible spectral disfavor and go straight to The Pines Restaurant, enjoy a complete Thanksgiving meal with none of the clean up? Hmmmmm.....sorry, Dad. Laziness has beaten down guilt.

113

Growing up, our home was always filled with friends. We lived on a large freshwater lake with bass so abundant they fairly jumped into your boat. Weekends were filled with barbecues and lots of laughter.

Of all my parents' friends, one couple left a lingering impression. I recall them as being elderly, but then to a twelve year old who isn't 'old'.... I do not now remember their names though they were often in our home. If I had to define them, I would say they were gentle people. Even in the midst of the crowds around our table, they alone stand out in my child's memory because of their small stature and quiet demeanor.

Setting the table was my job, and Momma said to never seat them apart from one another. When I questioned her about it, she would just say that they were most comfortable in one another's company. This intrigued me so much that quietly I began observing them. I understood that married people, like my parents, loved one another, but these two were different. Both my parents were huge personalities that each on their own could consume all the air in a room with their energy. Together they were dynamic, but stood quite well each on their own. This couple did not.

They seemed to operate as a single unit. I noticed that if either had to leave the room, the remaining partner seemed to wait anxiously for the return of the other. Helping Momma serve at the table, I saw that the little couple always held hands beneath the tablecloth. With the constant hubbub of jovial merriment that a crowd can bring, they seemed in a bubble all their own. They participated in whatever was happening, but it was obvious how in tune they were to one another. Seeing them lean in to share a word and a private smile, you could easily see that what each thought or had to say was infinitely more important than anything else around them.

They opened my eyes to a different kind of love. I'm sure the little couple, like my parents, have long since passed on. A wise woman once told me that if you are ever really special to someone and that person dies, then you aren't special to anyone ever again in that way. Understanding that as I do now, it is my hope that the little couple, who found one another so special, did not have long between their passings. For even as a child, I knew they would hate not being together even in death.

Loneliness comes to each of us at some point in our lives. For the elderly in an assisted facility who never receives a visitor it is a bedside chair that is forever empty. For a child, the loss of a parent leaves a vacancy at the dinner table and a hole in the heart. In a lengthy marriage, the passing of one partner leaves the other left to pull sadly alone in the traces.

My grandfather's Belgian horses, Jack and Beulah, had spent their lives together. They knew not a single day apart. When Beulah died, my grandfather said Jack wouldn't linger long without her. Within six months, Jack was gone. His loneliness was palpable.

The absence of that being who completes us leaves a Grand Canyon sized chasm in the heart. Whether the separation from them be of a short duration or eternity, loneliness follows.

Little of real value in life comes to us without a price. If you can count yourself fortunate enough to have known a great love at any age, one must then be willing to accept loneliness as the price to be paid when it is lost. As Alfred Lord Tennyson said, "Tis better to have loved and lost than never to have loved at all".

⚜⚜⚜

We humans have tribal tendencies. Whether from a need to be with others of our species or the necessity of protection from the dangers surrounding us. In the beginnings of man, we huddled together for warmth, communion and safety. Survival often depended on being one of a large group.

Early settlers to the west traveled in wagon trains hoping for safety in numbers. Circling the wagons has become synonymous with protection of any type.

Throughout my life I have experienced the comfort that circling the wagons can give. Though my girlfriends be far away, they have always reached out to circle the wagons of emotional support during my times of need. They are stalwart and steadfast in their support. They are my tribe. I am protected within their number, problems are minimized and their collective spirit lifts me up until I can find steady ground on which to stand.

One friend in particular I refer to as my "dead body" friend. She is the one you call when there's a dead body in your basement....without hesitation she comes to help, shovel in hand.

Almost everyone finds strength in numbers, in being part of a tribe, but for real back up there's nothing like a friend with a shovel!

Halloween makes me think of things that go bump in the night. As I see it, every now and then it's good to have the bejesus scared out of you. It gets the blood pumping and covers you in goosebumps.

I enjoy the decorations, the pumpkins and the frosty chill in the air. It's the one time of year that rats, spiders and witches get some really good PR. Their images and rubber forms fill department store shelves, grace magazine covers and take center stage in store front window displays in most cities and towns across the country.

In Ireland, ancient Celtic rituals celebrated Halloween as the end of the light half of the year. They had games, bonfires and fruitcake to celebrate. As I have an intense dislike of fruitcake, I can't imagine using it in any celebratory way.

Mexico has its Day of the Dead, and Romania has Dracula Day. Tourists can book parties at Count Vlad's Bran Castle. A night in Vlad's house might give you more than just goosebumps. In Italy, they celebrate with the Ognissanti. Red candles are put in windows, and an extra place is set at the table in hopes a departed spirit will join family members for dinner.

Halloween is a real treat for children. Dressing up like a superhero and dragging home a pillowcase filled with candy….a dream come true. One year I went trick or treating as Amelia Earhart. I donned an old aviator cap with goggles on my head and encircled my neck in a long white scarf. I gathered enough tooth-decaying candy to last me through the next year.

Spooky ghouls, goblins, ghosts and sacks of candy. Halloween is fast moving to the top of my favorite holiday list!

⚜⚜⚜

Something has disturbed my sleep. In the distance, I hear the plaintive howling of coyotes. Sliding my feet into furry slippers and wrapping a robe around myself, I step gingerly into the cold night air.

The October moon casts an eerie glow across the porch, front yard and the grassy field beyond. In the shadowy moonlight the forest creatures make known their presence. Chipmunks rustle through the leaves, and owls make a barely audible sound in their flight from tree to tree.

This fall night, temperatures have dropped considerably beckoning winter to come and stay awhile. I can feel transition in the air. Leaves everywhere are changing. Bright orange, yellow and rust colors are swallowing up the green. The fallen ones already carpet the ground and more will follow. Even now I see them spiraling earthward from the dizzying heights of my maple tree, glistening in the moonlight as they fall.

Shivering I pull my robe tighter around me, but I can't go in just yet. The beauty of this chilly night is spellbinding, and the world in slumber is missing it. Just as the earth signals its seasonal transition we, too, change.

Another year is drawing to a close. What my mountain was at the start of this year, it is not now, nor am I. The ebb and flow of life keeps us moving along with it. My bones feel cold now as misty night air settles over me. Going inside, I leave the moonlight and falling leaves to the creatures of the night.

⚜ ⚜ ⚜

In my life, no matter the year, the season or the place I am living and in spite of whatever current crisis is happening, one chore stays constant in my life….laundry. It matters not if I am well or sick, happy or sad…. the laundry must be washed, dried, folded and put away. It has become so second nature that I believe were I to lose my eyesight, I might still manage the laundry.

On the way home from the hospital after the birth of my son, I recall wondering how much laundry was waiting for me. I'm certain that as the plagues hit ancient Egypt, some Egyptian woman somewhere in the country was folding a pile of recently dried laundry. As the 1929 crash hit Wall Street, I feel reasonably certain that women all over New York were doing laundry, oblivious to the financial carnage happening in the business district.

Laundry is the gift that keeps on giving. Clothes are washed, dried, folded then put away, and almost before you can sit down you can feel dirty clothes hitting the bottom of the laundry basket. Even living alone I can sense the basket filling. Laundry is a vicious cycle chore.

Being of Irish descent, I hold on to the hope that the wee "little people" will one day take pity on me and magically take over my laundry chore. So far no sign of them.

Imagine the laundry nightmare in the Vatican basement laundry room….all those red robes discoloring anything white!

I cross myself just to think of it. I feel better reminding myself that at least I don't have pantaloons and dresses with yards of gathered cotton to be washed, dried and pressed with sad irons heated on a wood stove.

Just now I hear the familiar click of my washer shutting off, alerting me that once again I must transfer the clothes to the dryer. Lord, I do hope St. Peter doesn't ask me to help out in the laundry!

Moving to Sparta last December, I lived in a rental apartment awaiting the closing on my house in Glade Valley. The rear window afforded a view of fast moving water, a steep hillside beyond and one fairly good sized tree. A day or two after moving into the apartment, Sparta received twenty-two inches of snow. Talk about a mountain welcome! There were no leaves on the tree near my window save one. It clung tenaciously to the branch in defiant rebellion. Having only my clothes, my dog, and no television for distraction, I found myself monitoring the lone leaf's attempt to remain on the tree.

Coffee mug in hand, I sat down each morning by the window to see if the little leaf had survived another cold and windy night. Though facing extreme conditions, it managed to hang on day after day.

The original settlers to these mountains must have been equally as resolute. They withstood freezing winters and hardships we can only imagine. Yet they hung on, hunkered down and settled in. As tightly as the leaf was clinging to the tree, they held to their faith and their hopes. Here they built a life. I too traveled a long distance through life to come here. I was as eager to settle in and stay as those first settlers. Like them, once committed, there was no turning back.

Those first weeks in December brought cold temperatures and at times howling winds. The leaf held tight to the tree. I empathized with the brave little leaf. I too was alone and clinging to a branch of my own. A branch of hope. Hoping that at my age I'd made a good life decision to sell everything, pack up and follow my heart to move here.

As January 1st approached my house closing was scheduled, and I felt good that soon I'd be in my forever home. Packing up my few possessions in the apartment, I glanced out the window just in time to see the leaf let go and glide gracefully to the ground. Finally, in God's good time, it joined all the other leaves where they were destined to settle. Like me, I thought, coming home to roost. I'd been circling back here long before I understood the invisible pull always urging me to come back. Often we cling to a life branch not knowing the freedom letting go can bring. The leaf and I cling no more to a branch. We have let go and have landed where we are supposed to be.

There is a lottery in life with far more impact than the one people buy tickets for each week. A lottery so important there is no real gauge to rate how it affects the lives of everyone. It is the lottery of birth….it is a roll of the dice as to what sort of mother we each receive at birth. Everything about our future depends on the outcome of this important lottery. This can make or break a person. Our mother forms our first thoughts, attitudes, character traits and intelligence levels. As an infant we depend on her for sustenance. As a toddler her protection keeps us from harm. As a child her nurturing helps shape our personalities, and as a young person she guides us in the ways of right and wrong. Life may give us chances to excel, opportunities to see the world and allow us a multitude of options for career paths, but in this one very important "Mother Lottery", we have nothing to say about it.

Jacqueline Kennedy once told a reporter that if you bungle raising your children, whatever else you do doesn't really matter much. Looking back now from the safe distance of time, I review the job I did as a mother and wonder how my son would rate me. Did I make his heart smile? Did he feel protected, loved and wanted? Did the little boy with the toothless grin who held my hand and made me want to smother him with kisses when he looked up at me know how much I loved him? Did the young man I tried to protect from the ugliness of the world know the hopes and dreams I held for him? Will the grown man remember the books we read together, often the same one over and over because it was his favorite? I hope so. For I remember each and every giggle, lesson learned, every race he entered and most of the million questions he asked of me. I hope my answers then and now will guide him and serve him well, as I can no longer be a buffer between him and the harshness of the world.

As it is for everyone who comes screaming into life, I was his winning 'Mother Lottery'. He may have many friends, different cars, various jobs, change personal tastes and move to many different states in his lifetime, but he only gets the one-to-a-customer mother....and that is me.

Doubt and faith....more often than not, two ends of the same stick. Like lies told to protect and those told to deceive. Different ends, same stick. Love and hate, light and dark, innocence and guilt, ignorance and knowing. How quickly any of these can turn into the other. Everyone has a dual nature. Yin and yang, good and bad, sinner and saint. Some folks believe that literally on one shoulder sits a good angel and on the other a bad angel, perpetually urging us to have either good or bad actions. How exhausting would that be? I suspect it wouldn't take much of that to drive a person to drink or to madness.

Personally I'll go with the 'free will' theory. The chips fall as they may, and we are allowed the choice as to what we do with them. Always there's a crossroads....turn right or go left, stay or go back, stand still or run, say yes or say no. Seems life is filled with constant decision making. Could make one too afraid to get out of bed every morning.

The answer is really simple...my dad said that every dilemma that would ever come my way could be easily solved by asking myself what was the right thing to be done about it. That was his litmus test for everything. Think about it. It pierces right to the bottom line, leaves nothing to question and gets straight to the heart of any matter. Simple...in all things, do the right thing. I'm trying, Dad, I'm always trying.

Bob Newhart once said that when he dies, stands before God and is asked what he'd done with his life, he would answer, "I made people laugh". How, I wonder, will I answer that same question when put to me one day.

I have invented no new labor-saving device, discovered no disease curing serum, written no words of wisdom to be carved in stone, held no high office, built no monuments nor done anything so great it will be written about when I depart this veil of tears. I am a simple woman with little about me to cause notice and even less to boast about. With that said, what then will I leave behind? Perhaps the only child I had will remember me with love, my friends remember the joy of our years of acquaintance and those whose lives I may have touched will be thankful I crossed their paths.

Will the trees I have planted in these mountains sway in future breezes whispering my name and recalling me fondly? In future springs, will bulbs I planted color the landscape honoring my hard work? Will my ghost see the flowers of spring, bask in the warm rays of summer sun, watch fall leaves carpet the ground and in winter, waltz through drifting snowflakes beneath dark mountain skies lit by stars sparkling in the night like diamonds? I hope so. For this place cradles my heart, nurtures my spirit and heals my soul. Whether I am forgotten or remembered will be of no consequence, and I will go peacefully into the dark beyond if, as my reward, I am permitted to wander these hills eternally.

We are all waiting for Jesus to show up at our door so we can mete out our religious platitudes and dole out our Christian kindness as the need presented requires, but does God always present himself in as politically correct a manner as expected? I don't think He always shows Himself to us as a donation need caused by the latest hurricane, natural disaster or state sponsored relief quest.

We stop by the nearest donation truck to send canned goods to the Katrina victims, we routinely donate to whatever drive is brought forth by our respective churches and some of us can recall the last time we served food at our local soup kitchen. Of course these are all fine examples of our charitable natures at work, but recall, for a moment, how you felt the last time a homeless person approached you. Were you nervous, eager to move away, trepidatious that his closeness might either leave you with some disease or that he might, God forbid, ask something of you? Anxious is the way most people, myself included, if honest about it, really feel.

That bearded, odiforous, seedy-looking person who drags himself/herself by our office window each day, sits half unconscious on the bus stop bench as we drive by or the one we see riding his bike along the street...are they, in reality, God in our face? Just as God appeared three times to the rich man who had waited eagerly all day for God to come and dine with him, are we too waiting for the linen-robed, clean Jesus to approach us? Will our eyes only "see" Him when the vision satisfies our imagined idea of what He will look like?

As long as God doesn't "soil" us, we are charitable. As long as those starving children in Sudan are on our television sets and we can't smell them or hear them, it doesn't penetrate our consciousness. Is charity really genuine only when it is gut wrenching? Only when the pain we are relieving is palatable to our senses? I wonder if serving the leper is the only way God truly 'smiles' at our charity. Is man's inhumanity to man what God sees most in us? Is getting down and dirty the only way to really share our good will so that God will know we mean it? Does dropping a few quarters in the basket on Sunday from white gloved hands really "get it" in God's view point?

Today, here at work, one of these "biking, seedy" individuals showed up. I paused too long for my own personal comfort level in deciding whether or not to offer him a bottle of water. I cringe that I felt too anxious to go out to the mailbox where he sat eating a bit of food to offer him the water. What a sad commentary on my Christian heart and pitiful Christian attitude. Is my charity so shallow that it was stopped dead in its tracks by the stigma of poverty and the smell of reality? If I am appalled at myself, what must God feel for me today? It is one thing to say, "Please, God, if I have any blessings coming to me this day, give them to those more needy", but quite another to get off your ass and DO something for others. I am dispicable to myself at this moment. God appeared to me, and I let the opportunity almost pass me by. I did in the end redeem myself as the man came into the office to ask if he could throw away his trash. I then offered him the bottle of water. You see, God gave me one more chance, as He is prone to do. He practically had to shake me to get that charity out, but He knew it was in there. May God grant me another chance, and may I not pause as long next time.

❧ ❧ ❧

An old man passed away. His house was sold, and his belongings were divided and taken by his children. One of his daughters is my oldest and dearest friend. Downsizing her life and moving into a small condo, she gave me some items she would no longer need or have room to store. One of the items had been her father's....an old rake.

We all have our possessions and guard them closely. We tend to our things. We wash the crystal handed down in our family. Collectibles are purchased to add to our collections. They are dusted and organized. We store our things, box them lovingly when we move and take them with us. Our little treasures are unloaded into our new residences and placed with pride on display. All the things we treasure in life are scattered to the winds when we are gone. Death reaches out and one's lifetime accumulation of treasures is set on the front law in a yard sale. Old rakes included.

Mr Lind's rake found a loving home in my hands. An old adjustable aluminum leaf rake that was worn by the years is once again in service. As fall sets in, I find myself in my backyard with the old rake shaping leaves into mounds ready for bagging. I feel Mr. Lind is with me there in the yard. With each pass through the leaves, I channel him with my thoughts. He is conjured up through his rake. I wonder as I rake if he once again smells the odor of decaying leaves and that crisp smell of autumn that pervades my senses as I corral the leaves into small mountains. As I do the obligatory, seemingly endless fall job of bagging the leaves that seem to fall without cease in my backyard, I feel I am not alone.

A knowledgeable person on the subject of the Civil War, I recall conversations with him as we sat through many a soccer practice. I for my son and he for his grandsons. Concentrated on my task of leaf raking, my mind wanders to those conversations. They have come to my mind I am sure because I now possess his old rake. I realize in that moment that he may be gone to the world, but a part of him lives. Memories of him are alive to me through one of his scattered possessions. Perhaps we all live on lovingly in the things we leave behind. Even an old rake.

For most of my adult life, I felt like a part of my heart was missing. There was something lacking that no one, save myself, could see. I functioned quite well without it, but the void was keenly felt. I always knew the part was missing. I just had no idea how to fill it. I wasn't even certain just what it was that I needed. It was difficult to articulate even in quiet moments alone. It didn't always present itself as heartache - more like a void - a hunger that could not be satisfied. I tried to feed it, to satisfy it. But real fulfillment always eluded me. Oh, I tried....I married twice in my quest to silence the voice that kept me searching. But accepting a stand-in for the real thing always left me feeling that 'it' was still missing.

As a young girl I had a glimpse of the 'it' I sought. My parents' home was always filled with their many friends. An elderly couple that sometimes visited always captured my interest. They were unusual in that they were obviously still very, very much in love with one another and had apparently been so for fifty-plus years. They were quite enraptured with one another and held hands under the table. I caught them at this many times while serving supper round my mother's massive dining table. It was a standing rule that they never be seated apart. Mother said she thought they couldn't function as well when separated and that they had always been so. When one had to leave the room for any reason, the other could be seen to watch the door, anticipating their partner's return. I've never before or since seen two people who enjoyed one another's company as much as those two. Their great love and delight in one another left nothing missing from their hearts.

After turning fifty and divorcing yet a second time, I ceased searching. I knew my heart still had a missing part, but I had ceased longing after that which I thought was never to be found. My life had a happy stride to it. It was filled with friends, my garden, my son and my books. Times when the 'void' spoke to me I engaged myself in one activity or another so as not to have to address that which could not be fixed. Then, just like a story, the missing part found its way to my heart. A loving man harboring a void in his heart found me. He was the real deal. No longer does my heart yearn. My soul has found its mate. The abyss of void I felt has been replaced with a genuine love. No longer is there a missing part to my heart.

Cotton may be the 'fabric of our lives', but men are the 'heart of our lives'. They fill our lives with purpose and love. With delight and happiness….until you follow one into the bathroom. They do the darndest things that leave us wondering, "What could he be thinking?" The toilet seat is left up, a coffee cup left in a brown ring on a wooden table and underwear that almost makes it into the laundry basket. But we love them still.

When a relationship is good, the partners in our lives are our close confidants and dearest friends. They sit with us in emergency rooms and yet forget our birthdays. They bring flowers for no reason, but resent having to buy them on Valentine's Day because it's 'expected'. Attention is lavished on the details of polishing their vehicles, but they fail to pay close attention to a mood we might be having. Yet we love them still.

Each woman's complaints about the man in her life are as diverse as there are different men in the world. They go hunting for food that would be cheaper to buy at the grocery store. They fish for hours and catch nothing. They eat spicy foods knowing it will give them indigestion. They act macho in front of their friends yet brush away silent tears during sad movies. They wrestle equipment on hard jobs all day, yet dealing with our emotional needs is often too much for them. Still we love them.

Often they work with an irritable coworker all day perhaps for years and complain little. Yet if an evening out be scheduled on a game night, their complaints will be heard around the globe! They either work too much or too little. Some are overly ambitious while others are unbelievably lazy. Still hope springs eternal and we love them.

As girls we are weaned on the fairytales of perfect romance. We dream of a prince charming and usually settle for the average Joe. We find reasons to see and believe the best in them. Even in the face of evidence to the contrary, we often spend years working hard to make the best of bad 'men' situations. In spite of the difficulties, we love them.

My 'man' issues have usually stemmed from those 'prince charming' expectations. The man in my life now has met so many of my secret longings that I felt cheated when an expectation was left unmet. I thought that I deserved to get all the bases covered. That first flush of romance leads us to believe that the man of our dreams does not have feet of clay. But they do....each and every one of them. But somewhere in between the euphoria of new love and the reality of real life, we can find a balance. A middle ground of love and tenderness, common sense and fantasy, expectations and reality, dreams, hopes and mutual needs, desires spoken and unspoken, those met and unmet. In the end I found that the expectations took a backseat when I realized that I saw him clearly and that I loved him still.

⚜⚜⚜

Funny that the ending of a year on the calendar rolling over into the next should have become reason to celebrate. Especially in the manner we have adopted to celebrate it. Raucous parties, imbibing to excess, ridiculous party hats and loud noise makers.

The ancient Babylonians celebrated with a festival that lasted eleven days. Just imagine how incapacitated some modern New Year's Eve revelers would be if the parties went on for eleven days!

Our current partyfest is mostly due to Julius Caesar who fixed January 1 as the first day of our calendar year. The Romans celebrated with wild parties and the exchange of gifts. Thank goodness we dispensed with the gift giving as we Americans are usually too broke from Christmas gift giving to exchange gifts again a week later.

Personally I feel that somewhere in the past a Jose Cuervo relative had a hand in making New Year's Eve a drinker's dream celebration. In the same manner that Hallmark and FTD florists have invented holidays that require expensive cards and flowers....Secretary's Day....really?

I must admit that in my youth being at the center of a New Year's Eve party was crucial, but now I can no longer even stay awake to watch the ball drop at Times Square on television!

This year my nod to the New Year's Eve celebration will be to watch the moon shine over my pond, toss back a glass or two of wine and be asleep by midnight. On New Year's Day I plan to ring in my new year by cooking some black eyed peas in bacon fat and a pan of cornbread. Happy New Year!

All things change. Why then are we puzzled when love changes? Leaves change color in the fall, children grow up, baby teeth grow into adult ones, batteries in our remotes have to be changed, and even butterflies morph in the cocoon. Perhaps this change from passionate love to ordinary, everyday ho-hum love should be expected. Would Napoleon eventually have found Josephine mundane, lack-lustre? Would Superman have taken Lois Lane for granted? I wonder. Can we ordinary mortals never expect a superhero love to last in our earthbound relationships? Did Wonder Woman's husband in time stop hugging her during the night? Does Brad no longer desire to plant eager kisses on Angelina's voluptuous lips? Is this just what should be expected?

Perhaps complacency is more the issue here than lack of love. Just that everything changes from intense to casual to…dare I say…boring? Not because we feel less, but perhaps because we are too busy and tired to keep up the level of love's initial newness. I don't know the answer, but I do know I will feel the loss keenly if it comes. All that I do in my relationship stems from the feelings he brought out in me during the beginning of our relationship. Those feelings sustain me when I am tired or feeling low and keep me going. I don't want change in this aspect of my life. I realize that beauty fades, we grow older, we have ailments, all expected in life. But a diminished love is not something I want to accept or live with. I'd rather be alone. I formally protest against this sort of change!

Tires on my car need to be changed, leaky faucets are replaced, sheets are changed weekly, and career changes happen frequently now days. Gone are the days of spending thirty years at the same company. The family car no longer lasts long enough to be passed on to a family member. A mother's cherished table linens are not passed on to daughters anymore because they are no longer in vogue and young people don't iron anything. The long train ride experience to get somewhere is now passe as people want transportation to be as instantaneous as their communication. Life is fast now, and all things valued and cherished from years ago are for the most part no longer valued or important. Perhaps love has become lost in the fast paced new world. This new generation has constant change as a mantra. This new age fairly buzzes with perpetual change that seems expected, accepted and routine. I rail against all this change!

⚜ ⚜ ⚜

There is a thrill to be found in the small things life offers. Most passed over unnoticed, unappreciated. They speak to us though we often do not hear. Is life not made up of a thousand of these moments? Are we not the totality of those moments at the close of our days? Doesn't each breath, one upon the next, sum up our existence in the end? If we are judged to have been a valued friend, a faithful partner, a trusted companion, a good child, a great lover or a good parent, have we not lived a good life? If we have breathed deeply the sweet scent of a rose, laughed long and hearty and loved with a whole heart, have we not truly lived? In those moments has God not spoken to us?

Life is measured by our own personal yardsticks. When our ticket out is punched will we each not view our own pasts from our own perspectives and memories? Will the memories we each look back on sustain us in old age? Will they warm our hearts and give us pleasant glimpses at that which is gone but not forgotten? And will not those small insignificant moments that have made up our lives be remembered most? Days spent playing at the beach, a long walk through a lovely forest, a sunset seen from a mountaintop, snow covered peaks viewed on a solitary ski trail, the smell of a baby dusted in baby powder or a puppy snuggled in our lap. The minutiae of daily existence that in the end sums up a whole life. Common moments filled with uncommon magic.

'Twas a time when I was yours and you were mine. We shared a dream of love and sweet promise filled our hearts. We could not see and did not believe a divide would ever come. Loving eyes see only the here and now. With happiness ringing in our ears, we heard not the death knell tolling our demise. Ringing so faintly in the distance, it was easy at first to ignore.

So certain were we of mutual desires, stunned we were to find it not so. You pushed and I pulled back. The tug of war so tiring, it wore us out. You withdrew and I gave up. You didn't see me and I couldn't reach you. Watching it all slip away even worse than the final wrench of the end. Your silence I could not penetrate and my words were too much for you. You wanted more than I could give and your distance crushed me.

The flame burned out leaving embers that could no longer be fanned back to life. From our ashes rose one good thing. We did that well. He, the blossom left from the time when I was yours and you were mine.

❧❧❧

⚜⚜⚜

All round the house, melting snow drips out a slow rhythmic sound. The drip, drip tempo like the beginning of a concerto directed by Mother Nature. The sun so blindingly bright you'd swear summer was just around the corner. Light winds swirl the snow from laden limbs, and in the sunlight each snowflake gives off iridescent colors like Mardi Gras beads thrown from floats.

Winter is saying adieu to us. Not goodbye as she may not be completely through with us just yet. The sweaters, coats, gloves and hats will reside on their hooks by the door a bit longer. Boots stand at attention ever at the ready. But I feel the change coming.

Old bones creak a bit less as the temperatures warm slightly. Soon pots of beef stew and chili will give way to summer salads. Garden hoes and spades are as eager to emerge from my garden shed as I am to put them to work.

I plant a new tree every year when I'm fairly certain the freezes of winter are truly over. They are the children of my yard. I plant as large a specimen as I can afford and then nurture it carefully to insure it gets off to a good start. Water, fertilizer and more water. My trees are like the children we bring into this world, hoping to leave something of ourselves behind when we are gone. These trees will outlive me and I hope bring beauty and shade to this part of my mountain. Perhaps when future brisk winds blow through their sturdy branches, something of me will be remembered. My name may be whispered from one tree to another, and it will be recalled that I was once here.

Temper was something my grandmother considered a character flaw....especially if it couldn't be contained. Controlling her temper must have been fairly easy for her as I don't recall ever seeing her angry. I liked to teaser her by reminding her that even Jesus lost his temper with the money changers in the Temple. That cut no mustard with her.

Sadly, I have that bad character trait just like my dad. It is the genie you don't want to see come out of the bottle. I keep the bottle corked, but when it does escape, you better find a bunker to hide in. It seldom makes a prison break and when it does, I invariably feel ashamed of myself. When that internal switch gets thrown, there's no closing the floodgates on it. I am not proud of my character failing, but as it rarely makes an appearance, I seldom have to face its ugliness.

Cruelty to any being sets off a tectonic rift that I can feel bubbling up from way down inside myself. The ensuing seismic eruption is not a pretty sight, but I am powerless to put a lid on it. Perhaps we each have an 'Incredible Hulk' laying dormant inside us. Sleeping quietly in hibernation unless provoked. Each of us with an internal switch ready to be flicked to the 'on' position.

In history we have together fought wars in the name of righteous indignation. Brutality toward weaker beings made us determined enough to set aside our differences, to harness our collective anger and stand side by side against the aggressive oppression of tyranny. Like the chihuahua defending her young against a pit bull, anger can provide courage where there wasn't any and an internal fortitude previously unknown.

Perhaps, just this once, Grandma was wrong or at least a bit off the mark. Anger can be a good attribute when properly channeled and harnessed. Propelled by virtuous outrage, anger can move us to accomplish great deeds for others in need of our communal strength. It can lead us to demand attention on issues of importance and move us to make changes that right wrongs.

Personally, I'll try harder to work on my character flaw…to keep the cork on the genie's bottle and the switch in the 'off' position. I think Grandma would be proud.

After my mother passed away, well meaning family and friends expressed that they 'knew' how I felt. Hearing this left me with a strong desire to smack the next person who uttered those words to me. Feeling so distraught I was convinced that no one could possibly 'know' how I felt. Their kind words intended as comfort only sounded trite.

I was wrong. Anyone who has lost a mother does know some of the pain I was feeling. This pain knows no gender, social class or color. It is universal. We are never old enough to lose our mother. The mother/child bond cannot be denied. So strong it is said that a mother will override the natural instinct of self preservation to protect her child. It may be the most powerful bond in human nature.

The finality of death shakes us to the core, but the faithful have assurance that the spirit lives on and this brings comfort to many. Native American Indians believe that the deceased's spirit 'crosses the river' and walks joyfully thereafter in the spirit world. Tibetan monks believe the spirit leaves this world to soar blithely in the next. All pleasant prospects to be sure.

It has been said that memories are the garden of the mind from which we harvest solace in old age. Holding onto that, I have a kaleidoscope of memories of my mother to comfort and sustain me as I go forward without her. Treasured memories kept like pearls in a felt bag....taken out and remembered one by one when I need them. Treasured memories of a beloved mother that bring comfort to my heart.

Mother's Day is just around the corner. How do we really honor someone who gave up nine months of a year to give us life? Florists and restaurants are gearing up to cash in on the upcoming celebration of mothers. The first sound any of us hear is the sound of our mother's heartbeat in the womb. The first thing our fingers reach to encircle is one of her fingers. Our first nourishment is from her breast. As our eyes steady to focus, it is our mother looking down at us that we usually see first.

Native American Indians feel that they celebrate their mothers every day of the year, not just on the day designated to do so. They do not forget their mothers on the other 364 days. The Bible tells us that in honoring our mothers, our days will be long on the face of the earth. In the Cheyenne family unit kinship is very important, but the most sacred is the mother/child bond. Buddhism teaches that the unconditional love a mother has for her child can teach all of us to learn compassion for others. Personally, I found my mother's love so powerful that even death could not diminish it in my heart. She was my protector in childhood, my teacher always and would gladly have sacrificed anything to save me from hurt or danger.

Many people pass through our lives - wives, husbands, friends - but none leave such an indelible mark as our mother. Like it or not, something of her is seared into our beings. Her blood courses through our veins. A connection so undeniable that even if denigrated by another's barbs it cannot be lost, erased or forgotten. I know this for I, too, am a mother. So on this day, established by President Woodrow Wilson in 1914, let us honor any mother we are still fortunate enough to have with us and those who reside now only in our hearts, but live on in our memories. Happy Mother's Day!

Late in my life I finally met the man I was meant to be with. He came along at a most unexpected time and was not at all in my "life plan". As I had no intention whatsoever of falling in love or altering my patterns, I refused his overtures for a bit. When he would not take no for an answer, a great love began to blossom. One it scares me to think that I almost turned away.

As with all new lovers, our love was just as fascinating and thrilling even at our ages. We had first dates, first kisses and after a time first sex. His kisses made my knees weak and still do. He was and is all that any woman wants a man to be in her life. He is friend, lover and confidant. He makes me laugh and he gets my sense of humor. We enjoy time spent together even when nothing is said. An easy man to love and be loved by.

Like all new couples, he brought flowers…many flowers. With each phase of our relationship came a new reason to celebrate with flowers. A first month anniversary, a second and so on for the first year. Then came the first real year anniversary, then Christmas, Easter and of course, Valentine's Day. And the flowers that came for no particular reason at all…Just because, he said, he loved me. With each bouquet I saved the petals from every rose. I dried them and included all the petals in a very tall glass jar. As our time together grew, so did the petals in the glass jar.

As each layer was added upon layer, so did the memories I recalled any time I chanced to pass the jar. I remembered a special evening of a candlelit dinner, a surprise bunch he'd brought just to "make the house pretty", a birthday that would otherwise have been gladly forgotten he made delightful by walking through the door with flowers. He brought flowers and I layered them petal upon petal in the jar, adding memory upon memory. One day when he is too old to bring me flowers and I am too old to care, I will have my jar of petals and all the precious memories the petals recall for me.

❧ ❧ ❧

Rain has fallen all day today in a way to thrill all avid gardeners ...slow and steady. It is overcast and a bit gloomy. You called a few minutes ago and in that moment of hearing your voice, I had an onslaught of memories. That happens alot when I am talking to you. I am reminded of the way your black hair turning gray falls soft and curly about your shoulders in the morning before you corral it into a ponytail. Hearing you recalls your whispers in my ear as you sneak up on me in the kitchen wrapping me in your arms. The time you dropped to one knee with pink roses in your hands telling me for the first time that you loved me. So many thoughts flooded my mind in that moment.

You and I have had, by modern standards, a long run. We are compatible in so many ways it is almost scary at times. As in all relationships, there have been ups and downs. It is impossible to gauge the depth of love one person has for another. There are no measurements to accurately judge this feeling. But there comes a time in every relationship when the heart just KNOWS - there is a moment.

Your hands sort tools, lift ladders, throw cables, and still they reach for me with a gentleness that makes me smile. Your days are filled with running from one place to another and still you find time to call me. Nuzzling your neck makes me dizzy with your scent - a pleasant earthiness. It never ceases to surprise me that feeling of being out of balance when you hug me. It's sudden, fleeting, powerful and always - a thrilling moment.

A million times during the day thoughts of you cross my mind. You talk of your jobs, what you had for lunch and where you are going next. I enjoy sharing it all. In our life together, there are many mutual habits and hobbies. We share love and laughter in one another's company. Lives that were once individual have come together to form a couple. Remembering the past we've enjoyed, I look forward to sharing many more together moments.

✤✤✤

My mother died on a cold operating table during open heart surgery. As she was wheeled through the stainless steel double doors of the operating room, we said a few loving words to one another. We both knew these might be the last words we ever said to one another. A final goodbye.

On a day like any other, I took my loyal and loving dog to the vet for a routine teeth cleaning appointment. Not being back to his normal self at bedtime, I shut him in the sunroom and said goodnight. He died alone in the darkness of the night. An unexpected goodbye.

A pointless argument, raised voices, hurt feelings and a slammed back door. Love's wounded pride blinding me to rational perspective. I closed my eyes in anger and my heart to the love of a good man. A temporary goodbye.

A small boy grows into a young man. Kindergarten turns into high school in the blink of an eye. One day I am taking him by the hand into a first grade class, and before I knew it, he was driving down the street waving and leaving for college. A sad goodbye.

Goodbyes weave their way through our lives like a ribbon weaving in and out of eyelet trim on a summer dress. Not nearly as many a 'hello' to outnumber the goodbyes. Every goodbye a precursor to an ending - an era or a life. A signing off and a signing out. Always a final note…. Goodbye.

Life rocks along at a fairly common pace for all of us. A little faster here and there, but for the most part clipping along in step with the normal ups and downs of the average life. I am an average woman. I have an occasional glimpse at brilliance, but they are few and far between. I have never held aspirations of becoming a brain surgeon.

I felt my life was stumbling along fairly well except for the lack of a heartwarming love. I had resigned myself to the idea that the sort of love I longed for was only to be found in romance novels. I lived in a lovely home in a marriage lacking in the love I longed for. I wanted a love that would warm my heart and express itself in small things…a hand held for no reason, a hug while passing in the hall, a wildflower left on the pillow, or an arm around my shoulders sitting in the pew at church. These small things did not happen, and any spark of love I had slipped away.

My heart withdrew into itself until my son was born. A wee small thing of six pounds seven ounces came into my life and brought more love than I thought possible.

It is said that we should be careful what we ask the Gods to grant, for they surely will grant it. In moments of intense sadness I had prayed for love in my life. Loving my son was not the romantic love I'd longed for, but it was to be the greatest love I'd ever know. Those small things I had always imagined in my dreams of love now filled my days. A small hand reached to hold mine, hugs without number came my way, my presence brought squeals of delight, and his toothless little grin made my heart soar. Love had truly come in the small thing!

⚜⚜⚜

Every year at Easter time, an old outdoor drive-in movie theater near our home opened its rusted locked gates and became a huge open-air market. To a little girl trying to keep up with her daddy, it was a wondrous place. We arrived early and stayed late. Music sang out from speakers hung high on old light poles, odors of sausage and onions cooking on a massive grill assaulted my nose and whetted my dad's appetite. A sausage roll for him, and for me a corn dog on a stick.

This was my yearly big day out with my dad. Momma didn't come with us to the market....it was our day. As my grandma said, I could talk paint off a wall, and I suspect that my momma probably stayed home for a day of quiet.

I trailed after my dad from one stall to another, checked out the livestock, saw a man about a tractor he was selling and slowly but surely made our way around to the 'doll lady'. I had one doll, a Jenny doll. She was small and had come with a tall, metal pink and white case for her clothes and accessories. Daddy told me to pick out something special for Jenny. Daddy waited patiently for me to wander around the tables as the 'doll lady' offered selections. I remember being nearly struck dumb when looking up, I saw hanging on a tiny hanger a Jenny sized 'mink' fur coat. I pointed to the wee coat and looked to my dad for approval. He nodded, and I waited as he paid for my treasure. I don't think my feet quite touched the ground as we made our way back to the entrance gates.

Daddy said we had to take something home to Momma. We stopped at the chocolate vendor's stall. Daddy had the man cut two chunks for us off a slab of white chocolate so big you could roller skate on it. For Momma, he bought a large chocolate bunny. He laughed and said he knew she'd bite the ears off first....just like me.

As with every Easter, there was the requisite Easter dress, egg dyeing and hunting, and chocolate bunny ears to eat; but it paled in comparison to a day at the Easter market with my dad.

Almost everything in our pantry has an expiration date on it…. canned goods, bottled items, ketchup, beans and bread. Is there also an expiration date on love? Does love have a toss date? A "let this go before you watch it spoil" date? Just as mold sets in on a loaf of bread, almost from the moment it comes home it begins to go bad. Should each new love we encounter have an expected termination date or an…. "end this by:…….." date?

In the heated beginning of new love, it seems impossible to imagine the slow decaying that can happen. No matter how well kneaded and tended, perhaps it is only the way of nature that it will at some point go flat. Should love in our lives come with a change out or switch date?

Perhaps we can love too much. Like over kneaded bread dough….you can work it to death. I have heard that love is like flowers in the garden….if left untended it will die. But I can't count the number of times that I have overwatered a bed of flowers and lost most of them because of my overzealous care. Perhaps too heavy handed is as disastrous as neglect. Should love come with care instructions that spell out its needs like the care instructions on a mohair sweater?

All things give out. Cars rust, skin ages, joints wear out, fabric grows thin, hair loses its luster, light bulbs burn out…even our favorite espresso machine breaks down. Is it so hard to imagine that love could also diminish, deflate and expire as well? When love's expiration date comes, is there any way to get an extended warranty? Can its shelf life be lengthened?

When that white knight in the shining armor of love comes into your life, is it possible to keep him polished to ward off the inevitable dulling of his finish? Is there a way to keep him from becoming as ordinary as bread dough? As routine as my Catholic upbringing, fish on Friday night dinners? Can you love someone enough to hold their interest, their faithfulness and their joy in your company over an extended number of years? Is it too much to ask that love have no expiration date?

Hope springs eternal, and as a hopeless romantic, I feel that love can last forever. There is a combination preservative that can give love permanent shelf life....faith in one another, sheer determination to not fail, and unflinching, unequivocal, heartfelt love for one another. Love that comes with a label which reads, "daily care needed: provide many kisses, lots of hugs, and love without reservation. Expiration date: NONE"!

Office building lobbies have signs indicating the number of 'partners' within the different law firms. 'Partners in crime' is a common expression when referring to those engaged in mutually beneficial criminal exploits. Restaurateurs opening new establishments quite often have 'partners'. In Hollywood, movies are frequently produced by the 'partnership' of two studios. Dancers have 'partners'. Two scientists will collaborate as 'partners' to find a cure. Bridge games require a 'partner'. Webster's Dictionary describes a 'partner' as "a person associated with another in some activity of common interest".

None of the 'partners' so far mentioned will ever be so important as the life 'partner' you choose. Picking a person to walk with you through the trials and tribulations of life is a major decision, one often made at too early an age. We make this decision with no foreknowledge of the traits we might really need in a 'partner'. At twenty we don't know that a good partner will be a buffer against the arrows and slings of life's disappointments. For at twenty we know no disappointments. A youthful choice for a 'partner' might not include the trait of companion. For companionship would not be a youthful priority. The hormonal choice made in youth of a 'partner' lacks the wisdom of age. How would we know in youth what it really means to be in sync with another person? To know with certainty that your 'partner' has your back? That youthful choice lacks what only time can give us. Standing side by side with another through life's calamities is the only real test of your 'partner's' loyalty and steadfastness.

Shared common interests are often undervalued. Opposites may attract, but it is so difficult to live with a person of totally divergent attitudes. Another's habits are seldom considered when choosing a 'partner'. The habits of another can quickly grate on one's nerves, causing a fracture in the relationship. Sadly, we don't really know ourselves until later in life. So much changes in our personality, physical wants and needs, and life attitudes that choosing a lifelong partner is a gamble at best when young. What one wants at twenty is surely not the same at fifty. Yet the person I am in love with would surely have appealed to me at any age. I believe we would have aged well together. Like fine wine.

Fortune has smiled upon me and led me to someone who embodies the word 'partner'. We walk in step, side by side, arm in arm in every aspect of our commitment to one another. We are as perfectly matched as Bullah and Jack, my grandfather's Belgian horses. We walk as well in the "traces" of our lives as they did. Comfortable in our communion of spirit and attitude. What differences we have balance us rather than separate us. We are in sync and in love. We share wild-thing passion in the bedroom and crazy giggles over private jokes. He tells me the same stories over and over, and I listen delightedly with each retelling. He reads patiently the stories I write and tells me that each one is wonderful. I spell 'partner'.... 'R I C K'.

How do you tell of a mother such as mine who loved to fly fish more than anything? She was completely fearless, was the best cook and the best shot I've ever known, taught me how to gut a deer and sit like a lady all in the same breath, and by example showed me how to love fiercely and with every fiber of my being.

Laziness, giving up or whining was tantamount to mortal sin. She made quilts that won blue ribbons, sang like Kitty Wells and could clean and cook anything my dad brought home. She was devoted to my dad, and they were married 58 years. She was asked once if she ever thought about divorce in all those years. She answered, "Divorce no, but murder, yes".

She was 5'2" tall with bright red hair and a personality that lit up a room. People were drawn to her like moths to a flame. She sent out and received over 300 Christmas cards each year. The Sunday after Thanksgiving, we began the card chore. I addressed and stamped all the envelopes while she wrote something personal in every card.

Her parenting rules were simple and left no room for doubt....walk the line or deal with the consequences. I feared her more than God! She had such a big heart. She would give til it hurt and then give some more. In the end, it was her heart that failed her.

I will soon be the age she was at her passing. I am taller than she was, and I am more book educated, but never will I ever be half the woman she was. But because she didn't raise a quitter....I'll keep trying.

"If you are not for me, then you are against me" is an old, but tried and true expression. We spend our lives fighting against the world. Why would we continue to be with someone who is not 'for us'? Someone who does not in some way enhance our lives, make us a better person by our association with them, or bring joy to our hearts....then are they worth our time? Time being the one commodity we cannot replace. Once wasted, it cannot be gotten back. If your precious 'life' time is being sucked up by someone not worthy then you are truly 'casting pearls before the swine' as the Bible tells us.

The sales after Thanksgiving have people fighting to get into the stores. People are often trampled in the crush of shoppers, and some die. We go on Ebay to purchase something and fight the clock to make the final bid. People stand in line for concert tickets, and fights erupt as tickets run out. During hurricane season men have come to blows over the last pieces of plywood. In underdeveloped countries, food for starving people has to be dispensed with armed guards nearby so they do not kill one another getting to it. Men in the corporate world fight their way to the top. Starlets vie tooth and nail for a movie part. Babies travel the birth canal fighting their way into life. Mountaineers risk life and limb fighting nature and the elements in their quest to reach the top. Preachers admonish their parishioners to fight off Satan's temptations. Fight, fight, fight....what a battle life offers us. Surely a peaceful home life with a loving partner should be the norm. Unfortunately, not always. More often than not, partners I see seem as against one another as strangers elbowing to get on the subway first.

With all this human struggle, one would think couples would make every effort to create a harmonious home. Why do some spend their entire married lives in constant quarreling with their partners? The one place everyone would expect quiet, comfort and calm is the home. One's sanctuary against the world. The one place you can go to and close the door against all outside aggression, discord and mayhem. A fortress of harmony, tenderness and rejuvenation for the soul. And yet I know homes with such tension in the atmosphere it could be measured on the Richter scale. Couples strained against one another as tight as a rubber band in a slingshot. The slings and arrows of discord and unhappiness shot at one another with archer precision. Definitely each more against than for one another.

Observation of many couples left me in doubt that another existed who might share my views on the habitat required for couple bliss. Could there be a man willing to bring forth the effort to create and maintain such lofty expectations? And make no mistake, it does require effort. A willingness to bite one's tongue before an angry thought forms into words that cannot be taken back. A desire to put the other first even when it isn't convenient. Leading in all things with your heart for your significant other. Giving up self when the other's needs are greater. Creating a place for one another where comfort, calm and tranquility reign supreme. Building a nest together that keeps the fighting world at bay. A place to come to that shuts the door against all harm and allows love to replenish itself. A heaven in the midst of couple angst.

Just when I felt he did not exist, he came into my life. A man who asked God for the same thing I did….a person just right for me. Not just anyone was wanted….requested was the RIGHT person. I waited. After so long a time, I felt I had asked for too much. He waited. Eventually deciding that there just wasn't a 'right' person available. But good things do come to those who wait. Our thoughts and attitudes, similar on so many levels, have made us a compatible couple. We bring out the best in each other. Our love has made a safe haven of you for me and me for you. Our togetherness, a unique space where we are for one another against all odds and obstacles. In all things I know he stands in front of me to protect, beside me for strength, behind me for support and mentally always for me....never against me.

This night sleep eluded me, so I gave up and got up in the darkness to make coffee. Leaning against the porch post, my steaming mug in hand, I watched a bluish mist settle over my holler. It moved across the pond and up the hillside like swaying ghostly apparitions. Dewy dampness settled like a shawl around my shoulders and made me shiver. My bare feet felt the chill, yet I was rooted there watching what I would normally have slept through.

Life was awakening this day as it had since time began. It took no notice of me. Wind came off the mountain, swirling leaves into small eddies like ladies dressed in copper colored organza being twirled across a ballroom floor. A change was coming.

The earth was kissing summer goodbye. Fall would soon make a glorious entrance. Fall's real job is to prepare us for the cold to come when winter finally settles in. It also heralds the end of the previous year. A time for introspection, a time of taking stock.

Another year almost gone. I've noticed they go more quickly now. In the quiet of the coming day, my mind danced with its own apparitions….loved ones who have passed, old wounds if not forgotten now forgiven, love that was lost, missed chances and questions unanswered.

Morning was coming, pushing away the ghosts in the mist like the cobweb of memories in my mind. Nothing would hold back a new day. Least of all a jean-clad, barefoot gal clutching a mug of now cold coffee. Nature has no pause button. It rolls on with or without us. Turning to go inside it made me smile to think that one day my spirit may be one of the dancing apparitions twirling across the pond in this place I love so much.

❦❦❦

Recently, a flu bug settled over me, and during the night, the coughing had me searching for the oldest remedy I knew ….honey, lemon juice and whiskey. I prepared the concoction passed down from my grandmother and sat sipping it in the darkness as my mind wandered to a similar night long, long ago. My son was five or so and had come down with a bad cold. As the evening progressed, so did his fever. I had sat beside his bed with a pan of ice water rubbing his chest and head as he tossed and turned. Some time during the night, it rose to such a degree that he began to see birds in the bedroom. I filled the tub with cold water, and got into it with him. Returning him to bed wrapped in a giant beach towel, I lay there hugging him as he shivered with cold chills. I told him stories until he drifted off to sleep still flushed with fever, but better.

The bathtub scene repeated itself twice during that night, and Grandmother's cough syrup stilled his cough then as it did mine this night. I fell asleep that night sitting beside his bed on a stool, rubbing his forehead with a cold washcloth. I awoke as he stirred to find him staring at me in the morning light. "I love you, Mom", he said. "I love you, too", I replied, comforted by the fact that the worst was over. Had the cold bath and Grandmother's cough syrup healed him or had love? I'd bet the farm on love. Love had me in a cold bath tub pretending I loved it. It had me worried sick and running up and down the stairs filling the ice water pan as it melted, and had me rubbing his back until my arms ached. That night passed and many others like it, but twenty years later that same love keeps him constantly in my thoughts and prayers though he is many miles away.

This night Grandmother's cough remedy worked, and as I padded off to bed I wondered how many nights she had given her cough syrup to her sick children and spent the night beside their beds. The love remedy....it works every time....

We all race down the road of life at break-neck speed. Wishing for more, searching for the illusive, missing the present, dismissing the past and always certain that the future will be better. Then, in the midst of our whirlwind existence, life sometimes deals us a card we had not expected....illness. Even minor episodes of illness upset our apple carts. We moan and complain that a bad cold has sidelined our plans for an evening out or a weekend away. But a real illness can bring all life plans to a screeching halt. It tends to put everything in true perspective. We are reminded of our own frailty and are taken down a peg or two as my mother would have said. Ego is set aside, vanity is forgotten and pride is quickly shed.

Our health issues become paramount in our thoughts. It takes precedence over all other plans, concerns and decisions. That which is really important suddenly stands out in our minds as a red bird would in a murder of black crows. It seems we can see with clearer vision all that is around us. Those pesky details that seemed of major importance prior to illness suddenly reveal themselves as small, insignificant and irrelevant. It is during the siege of illness that personal backbone tends to come forth or not.

Some people pluck on an inner source of self reliance that enables them to deal well with the difficulties that illness presents. Others find strength in religion and family. Still others seem to crumble under the onslaught illness brings and fall into rapid decline. Not until faced with sickness can we learn our personal true colors. Our reaction to the calamity brought into our lives by illness is as individual as our fingerprints.

There are dimensions to illness that, until it rears its ugly head in our lives, we have not had to explore. Friendships feel the strain. Some friends step up to the plate when learning of your illness. They buoy your spirits, drive you to endless doctor appointments and even stay with you through hours of sitting in too-cold waiting rooms. That kind of friend comes to your aide without being asked, just as cream rises to the surface when butter is churned. Illness allows one to learn the true meaning of friendship.

Perhaps the best lesson illness imparts to us is that of love. We learn through illness that loving ourselves allows for calmness in the face of the storm it brings to our lives. That the love of good friends or a significant other lightens the burden of facing alone the often frightening aspects of illness. And finally, that in the end, when all that we are, have done and possess leave the scales of our lives teetering to one side, it is love that brings the scales back into balance. Love truly lifts us up when life's curve ball brings us down a peg or two.

What optimistic people we are. We buy lottery tickets for a month ahead. We plan vacations and purchase plane tickets six months before to get cheaper flights. Auto insurance gives us comfort that a future accident will be covered. Health insurance is a must just in case we need it down the road. Salon hair appointments are scheduled for the next month before the last snippet of hair clears the scissors and hits the floor for this visit. At our yearly teeth cleaning, we set up our next six month's dental examination. In January we fill in new desk calendars with all manner of appointments, birth dates and plans for the coming year. Email calendars, Blackberry calendars and cute kitten wall calendars all remind us of where and when we need to be in the future.

Little Johnny's soccer games for the whole season are booked on our calendars. Cute Janey's cheerleading camp is paid for in advance and marked in red for August of next summer. Oil changes are scheduled four to six months out or 5,000 miles, whichever comes first. Anniversary dates are circled and in tiny letters a week prior is "get gift". The A/C maintenance appointment is scheduled as well as the termite inspection.

All reminders of our future plans. Places we plan to go, meetings we need to make and scheduled events we dare not miss. I do believe if possible we would schedule our own deaths just so we might feel in control of that as well. Wouldn't that truly be scheduling the last big hoorah?

Gifts come to us even before we are born....a pretty face, a winning smile or even a charming personality. These gifts of nature come unbidden and as a child, unappreciated. A new baby's birth brings gifts from friends and relatives. Beautiful blankets to shroud the bunting in and bonnets to frame the wee face. Even Jesus received the gifts of the Magi upon His arrival....gifts of welcome.

From our first year on, birthdays ensure children a special day of gifts. Each year marking a coming of age in one way or another and age appropriate gifts to be enjoyed. Wonderful wrappings and splendid bows all ending up on the floor, marking the passing of another year....gifts meant to delight.

As adults, birthdays bring gifts that are more practical, anticipation of the day seems less than joyous and bears with it the feeling that it all might well be ignored. Almost as though a birthday party is more an imposition than a celebration. When does the adult lose the thrill over a day meant especially for him...gifts enjoyed with abandon?

As adults we can take back that birthday joy by celebrating not the passing of another calendar year, but by enjoying the one gift no one can purchase....the love of friends. So on that special day of yours, with all your friends around you, feel the love - not gifts in boxes gaily wrapped and beribboned, but in your heart, swollen to bursting because you are receiving the best gift of all....the gift of love.

There is a mystery that sailors in the old days feared. It was a mirage known as a Fata Morgana. It is a trick that fools the eye and the mind, brought about by an atmospheric duct of warmer air sitting atop cold seas. As I understand it, light is reflected off an object and is bent downward toward the cooler water near the surface of the ocean. Early seafarers feared seeing The Flying Dutchman ghost ship as it was considered a portent of doom. Though it was a mirage, their fear was very real.

I had a young cousin who late one evening was coming home through the woods. Hearing something following behind, his pace quickened. His heart began to thump in his chest, and as the sound drew closer he began to run. Racing as fast as bare feet could carry him through the woods, he crossed the backyard tripping on the porch step and fell flat on the porch. The thing was upon him….Jake, his redbone hunting dog, fell on him licking at his face. Fear had out paced his logic.

Fear comes to us all at one time or another and can take many forms. When my son was small, I feared crib death. I would rise during the night to lean over his crib to listen for his breathing. They say that seventy percent of our fears never come to fruition. I guess it isn't that we experience fear, it's how we deal with it that counts.

Catholic sailors crossed themselves against the evil of the phantom ship, and my cousin grew up leaving his childhood fears behind. For myself, I don't believe a mother's fears for her child ever go away….you just learn to live with them.

Is nothing ever easy? Does life have to be so hard? Why do some walk an easy path from start to finish while others struggle with every step? We are not all born equal! Even the path to heaven is fraught with difficulty. The rich man is given notice that his path to heaven is most assuredly difficult, narrow and almost unattainable. As difficult as a camel trying to walk through the eye of a needle. We struggle against the elements, the fates, social restraints and moral guidelines. For most, life seems a hard row to hoe. For those heavily burdened, gratitude is little more than a platitude.

Children starve in Bangladesh and need shoes in the Appalachian mountains. Soldiers come home from war in pine boxes, and mothers are given folded flags in compensation. The elderly sit forgotten in nursing homes waiting for death. Homeless shelters are filled to capacity. Children wait eagerly for adoption while childless couples wade through bureaucratic red tape. Welfare programs are drastically cut while millions are set aside to study a disappearing fish in mountain streams. Nice for the fish - unacceptable for the needy. The common man takes one step forward and two steps back. When much is lost, gratitude is a foreign feeling.

With so much angst, trouble, hardship and hunger in the world, I feel guilty for my contented life. I almost don't want to tell anyone about the wonderful man who loves me. I feel criminal for being so loved and in love. If I were not so deliriously happy, I feel sure that anxiety would overwhelm me. I am almost ashamed he has brought so much love to my life. Being Catholic makes guilt a second skin I wear like a mantle of righteousness. I pray the Rosary routinely, hoping to excise feeling too good about anything and reminding myself that Christ died to assure my eternal existence. I'm so guilty about my joy that I check twice before crossing the street for fear a car will take me out. As I don't feel I am a 'lucky' person, I keep waiting for the other proverbial shoe to fall. Surely this much love was really meant for someone else and I received it in error. Any minute now someone will come to claim him as being rightfully theirs. The bubble will burst, and I will awaken from this dream. I wasn't looking for someone to change my life, but he did….in ways I could never have imagined. He came to me as the embodiment of all I'd ever wanted in a partner. He was a crystallization of everything I thought a good man should be. As there are no real free tickets to ride, I wonder what my payment for such pleasure will cost. Disbelief overshadows gratitude.

Becoming more secure in this man, I find that I now pray my Rosary with a spirit of thankfulness. For all the world's issues, I pray for resolution. For all the needy, I pray for their fulfillment. For the lonely and lost, I pray for their deliverance. For the hungry of heart, I pray for them a great and lasting love. For the crushed of spirit, I pray for them solace. For those walking in the dark, I pray for light. For myself, I pray for acceptance of what I have been given. I pray for less questioning and more gratitude for what has been allotted to me. Be careful what you ask God to grant, for He surely will. I asked. He granted. I am grateful.

My garden and the work involved in its upkeep allows for considerable time to think. So much today keeps us from quiet contemplation. Today, as I watered the flowers, I thought a great deal about our love and our relationship. I realized that since we began our time together, I had begun to think of almost everything as 'we and ours and us'. No longer did my thoughts just encompass 'I, me and mine'. The slip in the fault line of personal life perception was quite a change for me. I had been self-centered. Not in a mean spirited way, but simply because I could be as there was no one else to consider in my life. This change in my life is akin to a shifting of the tectonic plates of the earth.

I was quite satisfied with the 'I, me and mine' lifestyle. I had no intention of altering either myself, my attitudes or the pattern of my life to accommodate anyone. Contentment had settled over my existence like an old and favored blanket. Then he came into my world, and it turned on its axis. Nothing has been the same since. My decisions are no longer based on strictly my needs and wants. I now buy groceries with him in mind. He is in my thoughts as I purchase a new dress. My heart beats now in tune with his and I love it. The 'us' in my life has made me a better person.

In the small things and in the larger ones, I find myself thinking of his needs before my own. Pouring his morning espresso and taking it to him is sheer delight. Sitting down to watch tv, I check to see if he has a glass of water. Saying a quick Rosary as his car pulls from the drive is done automatically. Concerns for myself now pale in comparison to the ones I have for his welfare. Little things I have learned that please him give me the greatest pleasure to do for him. I have found that my heart and my life are enhanced in giving to him. The 'us' he has brought to my life has made my spirit more giving.

It has been said that the greatest love is in giving of oneself to others. It seems to be something we think of in global terms, not relationship terms. But what greater measure is there of love than the happiness you bring to your partner's life? Why shouldn't this grand scale of love's measure be scaled down to the smaller picture of day to day life? Where better to start giving of oneself in a generous and loving manner than one's own partner? The person we have vowed to love, honor and cherish. Today's world greedily encourages the 'I, me and mine' attitude. Totally opposite of what nurtures a loving relationship. If the 'us' at the core of any relationship is to prosper, the 'I, me and mine' must take a backseat. Where once my life was an 'I, me and mine', there is now a loving 'us'.

Several years ago I purchased a small, antique child's school chair. It is worn from age and use and has not a single drop of its original paint on it. In the antique market, I had walked by the little chair several times, and with each pass it seemed to 'speak' to me. It needed a home and I brought it to mine. I have placed stacks of books on it, potted plants, and moved it all over my house in search of the perfect spot for it....the no longer homeless little chair.

A neighbor recently told me the little chair was so worn out I should trash it. I cringed inside at her words and politely explained that I loved its worn patina, and that I could only imagine the stories it could tell if it could but speak. My neighbor's careless remark had flushed me with a surge of maternal instinct to protect my tired little chair....the lonesome little chair was alone no longer.

The wee chair's exterior sometimes reminds me of a close friend. How often does someone's exterior demeanor belie a completely different interior. My dear friend has such a pleasant smile, but her eyes are sad. Her internal patina worn and tired....like the little chair's oak legs....strong, but no longer able to bear a heavy burden.

Like all of us seeking our place in this world, I feel the little chair was in need of a place too. Aren't we all looking for a soft place to fall, arms to encircle us and a sympathetic ear to listen? We all hope our lives will settle into a familiar pattern, a comfortable nest and someone to love us. What more could we or a tattered little chair ask from life....like myself, the little chair has a home and someone who loves it.

There are many types of last words….umpires at games have the last word… "OUT!", or better still….. "SAFE!". Poems have been remembered for last words. Who does not know Poe's "The Raven" and its final frightening "Evermore"? Speeches have moved nations with their last words….Kennedy's "Ask not what your country can do for you…" and of course….MLK's "I have a dream". Churchill's "we shall fight them on the beaches…." led men into battle. Everyone remembers those moving final words. Words that punctuated great speeches, that moved nations, promoted change and altered history.

Great men have often left us with final last words. Robert E. Lee was quoted as saying, "Strike the tents" on his deathbed, referring to troops breaking down camps on the battlefield. Stonewall Jackson left us with, "Let us cross the river and rest under the shade of the trees". Julius Caesar's "Et tu Brutus?" comes immediately to mind when famous last words are mentioned. The Bible gives us its shortest verse in two small, moving words…. "Jesus wept". Final thoughts, final words, in final moments.

Having the last word is often the goal in arguments…lovers don't want to be the last to say the final goodbye on the phone, and the last words in great novels stay with us forever…. "Frankly, my dear, I don't give a damn".

Life has its own heart stopping, life changing and final words… "It's a boy!"…. "there's been an accident"….. "I do" …. "You're fired"….and….the ones none of us wants ever to hear, the most final of all words…. "it's terminal". Words that echo in our heads and put our feet on paths not expected.

As I contemplated 'last words', I wondered what our last words might be to one another. If final moments allowed, surely the expected…. "I love you". That would slip from our lips as easily as it does a hundred times a day when we are together. But there are other words I would want to leave you with… "thank you" for all your love has given to me and for all the best you've brought out in me. I would want to remind you that it is not "goodbye", but only "adieu" for this life is but a stepping stone into another in which I hope to see you again. Perhaps for us a secret letter code will do as well as a page full of words…. ILUA….always.

Once again the calendar brings us round to Valentine's Day. It is February and cold, yet I am warmed by the thought of love. I pondered the many forms love takes throughout our lives. We have all heard of young love, puppy love, new love, crazy love, and mature love. I contend that there is yet another 'love' …..contented love. The love that comes on the other side of all the others. That love that fits like a well worn pair of slippers or a second skin. That kind that comes from feeling totally secure with another person. A closeness born of mutual respect and admiration. As though that other person fits you like a reflection of yourself. A mirror of your thoughts and attitudes. A closeness that finds you finishing one another's sentences. So in tune you almost read one another's minds. A love that rivals the connection of twins or even the mother/child bond. Love that binds, is abiding and has a communion of spirit like no other. Connected love.

This is a love that perhaps comes only later in life. Later when you have learned that there is no competition with a partner. When you have learned that cooperation and mutual goals are the glue of commitment. Love that has a backbone of sharing and pulling in the traces of life together. A love that knows that the weight of the wagon is lighter when two pull in tandem. Committed love.

In this love, the other's needs usurp one's own in all things. Finding the fulfilling of the other's need before your own is an easy, unconscious habit. Looking for ways to please each other an underlying theme in the relationship. This love that I speak of supports and uplifts its partner. It nurtures and encourages personal growth and delights in one another's accomplishments. Protecting one another from danger from the world and ennui from within. Giving love.

Love so secure lays the groundwork for mutual passion. After years the heart still beats rapidly when your partner enters a room. A joy in one another that knows no bounds and provides a playing field for mutual delights. Sexual love.

A love like this sees you as you are and loves you still. It encourages you in all endeavors and comforts you in disappointment. This love creates security, brings joy, satisfies the soul and body, and engulfs one another in a cocoon of safety from the world. Truly, a contented love.

❖❖❖

Each day dawned anew, and he rose to put one foot in front of the other until he had managed another day checked off the calendar in the kitchen. He used the same calendar she had used. It had her handwriting all over it. It still told him their children's birthdates, her hair appointments and meal plans she had for Sunday dinners. It was another small item that kept her near him.

Time loomed each day in front of him....long and lonely. To keep old ghosts at bay, he kept as busy as possible. As busy as his old, tired bones would allow. He still pruned the trees in spring, the hedges in summer and raked golden leaves in fall. Snow blowing had become a real challenge. After a bad fall, his children had paid a service to clear his driveway during the winter. He still managed his own laundry and could cook a tasty pot roast. He still drove himself to the grocery store and to doctor's visits. He knew the routines of his neighbors, his postman and the paperboy. He had lived so long in this house on this street that he was a familiar figure to everyone. All during the day he followed his routine of activities, but the nights were the hardest for him. Sitting alone in the evening brought him face to face with his memories and the sadness he held back during the day.

After the death of his wife, he had stubbornly refused to leave or sell the house. What no one understood was that for him, she was still there. He alone could see her standing at the kitchen sink, walking down the hall or sitting beside him in the front room at night. They wouldn't believe, even if he told them, that she lay beside him each night in the bed they had shared for 46 years. He felt her presence most in that room.

After the funeral, everyone was insistent that he empty the closets of her clothes. The night before his daughter came to help him with this chore, he'd hidden some of his wife's things. Her nightown he kept folded under his pillow. He could bury his face in it and literally conjure her presence in his mind. So real was it sometimes that he would still reach out to touch her.

Sundays were difficult days for him. Gone were those lazy afternoons spent puttering around the house with her. Even with different projects to do, her presence made him comfortable. He missed that most....just knowing she was there if he called out to her. Now his Sunday afternoons were spent at her grave. He weeded and put flowers in the vase. Silk ones usually, but occasionally when his heart ached more than normal, a single red rose to show her he loved her still. Standing there he often spoke to her. Of big things and of small he talked on and on to her. If anyone had heard him, they would surely think him mad. Mad he was not, but lonely for her he was....constantly. Day to day, week after week, minute to minute....he missed her. It is said that time heals all wounds, but for him in the years since her death, his heart bled sadness with every beat. His aching for her was palpable. At night it stung him as it engulfed him in the darkness.

Often his thoughts wandered to the first time he'd seen her. The smile on her face had lit up his world. He could still remember the way his knees had felt like jelly at the sight of her. He knew immediately that she was "the one". All through the years that feeling had never wavered. If she were away even for a few hours, he felt a rush of joy at her return. His sons often teased him about finding another woman, and he was occasionally introduced to 'eligible' ladies from his church. All of this he found amusing, but for him there could never be another woman. He'd

176

given her his heart and with her it would remain. The love he felt for her left no room for someone else....there could be no replacement...ever. He was content to wait to see her again in God's own time. He was certain to the very marrow of his bones that they would be together again. Until then, he would patiently put one foot in front of the other, checking off each day as it passed on the kitchen calendar and ....wait.

All in an instant his dark skin looked pale, his hands shook a bit, his face appeared to be clammy and he was dizzy. I rose from the chair where I had been sitting, and he sat down. I sat still on the foot stool and watched as the normal color returned to his face. The lightheadedness disappeared, and the shaking stopped. It was all over in a few minutes. In those few moments, I felt the raw exposure of thoughts none of us likes to think and certainly don't want to examine.....Love given and love taken away.

Those few moments brought flashes of what my life would be without him. I did not need to feel what his loss would mean to me to know how much I love him. Every morning that my eyes open and each night as I drift off to sleep, I am aware of that love and what it means to me. I am thankful. He is always so strong and I rely on him so much. I am grateful for our love. But in that moment, I realized that nothing I could do would hold him here. How quickly he could have slipped away from me....Love taken.

They say that before your own death, your life passes before you. In that moment watching him I saw in a flash all the wonderful times we have had together. It was all so fast it seemed impossible to have had so many thoughts. They all flooded in together, all jumbled up and moving through my mind in snatches of memories. My heart ached as it pounded in my chest. So much love we feel for one another....Love given.

Very quickly he felt himself again. It was only a blip of time and we moved on with our evening of habits and dinner preparation. The shadow of how I'd felt followed me as I moved about the kitchen. All returned to normal. He took the trash to the curbside and came in to wash up for supper. Nothing appeared to have altered. Except I knew those few moments had given me a new perspective. I plan to appreciate our time together more. Ours was a love truly given and could in a moment, be taken.

There are keys to the city, the car, the front door, back door, and Uncle Bill's old trunk in the attic. There are keys to the kingdom, zoo cages, gates, cabins, safety deposit boxes and storage units. Each important in their own way, but none so valuable as the key that unlocks the heart. The key held by that special person somewhere in the world who is meant just for us. For some, finding the key is a lifetime quest. That special key that unlocks every dream, desire and yearning. The key that unleashes boundless joy, love and happiness. This key is a bit like a glass slipper. It must be an exact fit to truly unlock the heart. This key sought after and longed for but sadly remains elusive to many.

There are places in the heart accessible to only the most sincere. Places kept under phantom lock and key. Dreams kept under wraps, untold and unfulfilled. Many kept hidden for years. Some even for a lifetime. They are kept alive by secret longings of what could be. They surface now and again only to be crushed by life and disappointment. And still they hang on tenaciously. Clinging to the hope they have not been dreamed in vain. Secret visions of the perfect soul mate. Longings in the soul so deep the Grand Canyon pales in comparison. The imagined love in the heart so different from the reality of the emptiness that exists. The heart shut down so long the key thought lost.

People cross our paths and touch our lives in ways unexpected. Just when the heart has bolted the door, someone comes along with the key. Someone loves us, and a life change occurs equivalent to the shifting of tectonic plates. Love that longed to be given is released as if floodgates were opened. A contentedness settles over the heart like the warmth of sun on a cool fall day. The spirit is lifted and a purpose settles in the soul. No riches on earth can provide the thrill of love given and love received. The heart glows as brightly as the lighthouse beacon seen by ships at sea during dark nights. Love spreads out from the heart like ripples made on the water from a tossed pebble. The difference colors everything in your life. Unlocking the heart opens it to new possibilities, deeper compassion, and greater forgiveness. The quest for the Holy Grail was no less daunting than a lifetime search for someone possessing your 'key'.

What greater gift than to love and be loved? Who do you thank for such a gift? God? Fate? Cupid? To fully grasp what a gift it truly is, just remember life without it. Sadly wishing you had someone to share a morning cup of coffee or an evening glass of wine. The yearnings of dark nights with no arms to encircle you. Wishing there was someone with you to celebrate an accomplishment. A good book read and no one there to share the story. How much better favorite programs are when watched with someone. A person to share your interests, joys, disappointments, desires and love is a rare find. Somewhere in the world is a key that fits every lock. I found mine.

❦ ❦ ❦

Early this morning I rose to find ice on the pond, snow on the ground and air so cold my breath wafted out from me in curls of hazy fog. Tree limbs were laden with snow. Every so often a clump dropped to the ground making the only sound I heard.

Standing on the porch I felt quiet serenity fill my soul. My spirit settled in communion with the peacefulness of the moment. A chipmunk, oblivious to my presence, ate from my bird feeder, filling his chubby little cheeks. My small slice of mountain heaven was blanketed in a shroud of white. The earth in stillness awaited a new day.

Soon all life on the mountain would awaken and the spell of peace be broken. Life would intrude. But for a dreamer like me, there's always the hope of another such morning. When snow will again dust the landscape like cake icing, the earth will close in on itself in quiet introspection like my own, and the beauty of such a moment will move me as nothing else can.

Perhaps if I memorize moments like this, store them in the vault of my mind, one day, when my eyes fail me, I can mentally relive them. I once heard that memories are the garden of the mind from which we harvest solace in old age. The older I become, the more I understand that.

All his adult life he had lived in this house. It was really the only home he'd known. His children were raised there. All he knew of home, hearth and family was wrapped up in the mortar and bricks of it. His wife had chosen the colors for the walls and decided where to place the furniture. After her passing he'd left it all exactly as she'd left it. The familiarity gave him comfort against the sadness of being without her. The house had become his solace.

Another year had come and gone. The holidays were just around the corner. Sitting in his easy chair with snow settling against the window panes, he could recall each and every past Christmas. In the evening stillness he could see all those past Christmas trees. Beneath the twinkling lights lay the children's presents. So many, many presents. He'd always wanted them to have all that he had missed as a child. The house was his memory bank.

All through the years he'd replaced, repaired or painted anything that showed age on the house. He had been caregiver and caretaker for it. Now it was the house's turn to care for him - to wrap him in a blanket made from a patchwork of cherished memories....his wife standing at the kitchen stove, his little girl dressing her dolls on the living room floor and the boys bursting through the back door always on the run. The house was his sanctuary.

Being alone had become more difficult as the years passed. Old friends slipped away, long time neighbors moved, his favorite local pub closed and his long time postman retired. Keeping up with the yard work had become a chore and dealing with winter snows a challenge to say the least. But here in this house he would remain. For in the embrace of its walls, the house held his vision of the past, tender thoughts of his loved ones and all the precious memories of a life lived under its roof. Mingled there in the walls and the rooms, from attic to basement, the old house was his heart.

A friend recently asked me, "Where, at 58 years old, am I supposed to be?" Her question started the wheels in my brain spinning. It was a personal question that applied to all of us. It titillated my brain cells….questions arose and answers responded….which in turn brought more questions.

Starting out on a trip, we set the auto navigation system and are told where to go and when to turn. Life does not give us a destination plan. We start out, run the course and find ourselves at the end. Only then are we able to clearly see turns here and there that might have set us on a better path had we but taken them.

There are blueprints for new homes designed to show us where every board and rafter should be placed. Triple A Auto Club lays out trip plans that direct your travel route. Manuals are written for automobiles that locate every belt and gear for repairs. Boiler rooms for large industrial complexes have schematic diagrams on the wall enabling workers to locate trouble spots quickly.

Is there really no architect for the life plan of man? Are we really thrown out there to decipher the signs and stumble our way along the road of life with little to no guidance? Are we simply at the mercy of the experiences that shape us as we roll along our life journey? Leaving us to question what our purpose is and where we should be. As I pondered these questions, I thought of myself and when I found my answer. My path had been an ordinary one. It had educated me, blessed me with a good child, and had settled late in life to a comfortable pattern of good friends and simple pleasures of home and hobby. I thought I was where I was supposed to be....until I met the love of my life. He has shown me the simple joy of life in his company and of love in his arms. My destination is reached, wondering if I am on the right path is over, and I know I am where I am supposed to be.

It is said that death takes a holiday and people go on break. There are leaves of absence and bears hibernate. Ducks migrate south and monks have retreats. Teachers take sabbaticals and Austrailians go on walkabouts. The religious make prayerful pilgrimages and the distraught get away to 'find themselves'. Even meditators levitate their minds to a distant realm and psychics transport themselves to an 'alternate space'. So does love need distance too? I mean real, heart stopping love. That sort of love that makes your gut hurt when the other person is gone even for a short while.

We step back from our work and are said to 'regroup'. But does a real deep, abiding love desire a "timeout" from the object of that love? If you love someone so much that you feel an amputation has occurred when they are not with you, how can distance be sought? If someone means more to you than your own next breath, why would you want to "retain your individuality"? Is independence what one would really seek if true love had been found? Perhaps 'alone time' has been glamorized into something more than it really is. Does heart stopping, genuine, 'can't live without you' love ever really need down time, timeout, a hiatus or a break?

We are told that the intensity of love changes over time. but does it really have to? If you can pump up old bike tires, why can't romantic love be revitalized with a blast of romance? Love doesn't have to lessen just because time goes by. Wine ages and becomes more special as time passes....why not love? Does the thrill really have to 'be gone' as they say? We take vitamins to pump up our vitality....why not love vitamins to revitalize love that has hit an energy slump? Like muscles that have atrophied and need exercise, love sometimes needs a boost.

Led Zeppelin moved my soul in my early days. That feeling has never left me. At times it has been buried in the tedious details of a life lived. We get busy, children come and with them their needs. As a woman you put aside yourself and work at pushing them forward. Their needs take priority over everything in your life. Suddenly all your work is done and they leave. The music returns to the heart and once again we find time for ourselves.

Having regained myself, I started a list of those things I always said I would do. I taped the list to the fridge, and it hung there a few days. Everytime I walked through the kitchen, the list nagged at me. I had written the list, now I needed to move my ass and get started DOING.

First on my list was to get a tattoo. I did not have to look at the design books in the tattoo parlor. I knew and had always known exactly what design my tattoo would be. It would be the four symbols from the ZoSo album by Led Zeppelin. The band members had each chosen a symbol that meant something to them. Those four symbols combined meant something to me. They represented a time when I was totally free to be me. Perhaps they represented me at my best. I knew no one would understand, and most would think it foolish. But I got it just for me and I would always know why I chose the design I did.

No matter how old I am and how wrinkled my skin becomes, when my hand goes to the middle of my back to that small area below my waist, I will touch my tat. In that moment, I will be transported to the first time I ever heard Robert Plant belt out a song that sent shivers down my spine and made my knees go weak. I will hear again John Bonham make his drums scream from the violent pounding he gave them. In that brush of my hand across my tattoo, I will feel the hairs stand up on my arms as I mentally hear Jimmy Page play his guitar with a violin bow. John Paul Jones will fill in the background music of my memory trip.

Some will think my tattoo a fanciful tripping of an older woman reliving her youth. But they would be wrong. I need no inked tattoo to bring Led Zeppelin to life, for they live in me all the time. They blare away in my car while I drive, house cleaning goes ever so much easier with them pounding out a beat, and passionate bedroom fun is always better with Robert Plant in the background! My tattoo is a visible symbol for something magical….the music that became the thread weaving its way through the years of my life. On my lower back in black ink….Led Zeppelin lives!

❧❧❧

A popular song told us the story of 'Big John', a coal miner dying to save the lives of fellow miners during a cave in. A generosity that saved lives and cost him his own. That 'Big John' was said to be a physically tall and large man in size. But in life there are others of such stature in spirit who step forward constantly to help others. Perhaps not supporting timbers in a collapsing mine, but helping make the lives of those around him better. Always caring….our Big John.

The 'Big John' in our family has always been there to keep the wolf from the door of grandchildren who are not yet on their feet. A 'big man' who steps forward to aid older neighbors who can no longer mow their own grass or shovel snow from their own front doors during harsh winters. A 'big' man who spent his life doing for others in whatever crisis came to the family. The man who took over funeral arrangements when others couldn't handle the issues laid on them by the death of a loved one. Always there with a shoulder to lean on or help you push if your load was too much to bear alone. Generous to a fault…the man who would literally give you the shirt off his back….Big John.

He is that person who assisted when a hot water heater needed installing, a garage door went on the fritz or an air condition wasn't working quite right. No task was too great or too small for his help. Neighborhood children remember the fun fellow who, on the first day of summer, tossed quarters into the pool for them to dive in and find. That all round good guy who takes charge and gets things done. The one in the family who is called because you know that he will know what to do, how to do it and equally as important….do the job right….Big John.

I drove by a church today, and the sign out front told me that there was no greater love than the love of the Father for his children. Speaking of course of God's love for us, his children. It caused me to consider how affected we each are by the love or lack of love from the fathers in our lives. A mother nurtures and cares for the infant, but as we grow, our life path is surely in great part

189

affected by the actions and examples of our fathers. The 'Big John' in this family did the job right. He stayed the course, applied himself to the task of fatherhood and raised three fine children: a caring, loving daughter and two sons with personal principles and honest natures. He often worked three jobs to support his family and never wavered from his duties. A good man of big spirit and even bigger heart…Big John.

The Great Wall of China was built to keep out great hoards of marauding infidels. The Imperial Palace in Japan has high walled gardens ensuring that quiet meditation and silence are protected from outside noise. The Berlin Wall guarded Communism from western ideas. Ancient Irish castles had great stone walls encircled by moats protecting the inhabitants from warring tribes. Western frontiers ensconced settlers behind wooden forts, protecting them from savage Indian attacks. Modern yards are fenced to keep luscious lawns from wayward foot traffic. Jericho was a walled city mentioned in the Bible.

But no wall ever erected, no matter how tall or how thick, will ever be as impenetrable as the wall we can build around our heart. We put up all manner of barriers to keep love from hurting us. Once stung by love's piercing pain, we build a wall of protection around our heart only the most determined can topple.

I built such a wall. I was justifiably proud of its ability to protect me. I prided myself on its functionality and clever design. Time and again, it rebuffed assault from the best men my town had to offer. My wall protected me from glowing, feigned admiration and insincere flattery. It ensured my safe distance from all phony suitors. My wall had a built-in alarm system second to none. Safe Touch Security paled in comparison. Surely the White House could boast no better protection! It would sound the alarm of caution when my defenses might be at a low point, and it kept me safe. My walls also isolated me and caused me to seem unattainable. In my eagerness to protect myself, I set myself apart.

Until a true knight finally came to me. He wore no armor. No mantle of chainmail covered his body. No glistening sword of steel hung at his side. He sat astride no white horse. But just as a knight of old laid waste to the walls that encircled a castle, he broke down the barriers surrounding my heart. He laid siege to the gates that were barred and locked. Against all manner of odds he would not take no for an answer. He untied the ribbons that held up my long hair. The flowers he brought were beautiful, and his expression of love sincere. With the truth of his words, he released the chains that bound my soul. He brought sunshine to my walled-in heart.

From a long way off I hear it before I am even conscious that I am listening for it….the train whistle. That long, lonely, plaintive sound that long ago beckoned dreamers and hobos alike to ride the rails and see the country.

In years gone by, hobo junctions sprang up in places where the train slowed, and men could easily jump into an open car. During the Great Depression, the trains rocked along carrying those men in hopes of finding work in other parts of America.

As the train slows to come through the intersections of my side of town, I am reminded of a slower time when people wanted to see where they were going and enjoy the passing scenery through a dining car window. Now days life moves in a blur of rapid information and immediate response. We have no time nor patience for anything slower than a nanosecond. I wonder how the trains will fare in the brave new world where ambling along is considered antiquated.

At the railroad crossing a few days ago, I came to a stop just inches from the cross arm. I watched and listened as the old train swayed and lurched its way along. It was a freight train carrying goods and materials across the land. So purposeful in its journey that I was reminded of Thomas the cartoon train and smiled to myself as I continued to count each car as it passed.

It is during the night though when I am restless and awake that I feel the most empathy with the lonesome sound of the train whistle. Hoping I'm rolling down the right track in my life and that I am taking every opportunity to enjoy the scenery as I go along....for as we all know....the ride can be very short.

❀❀❀

We schedule everything in our daily lives. Everything, that is, except love. We take all manner of care to eat healthy and exercise to help our hearts stay fit, but we don't think much about the emotional wellbeing of our hearts. Love, like death, cannot be scheduled. Love's timing cannot be ordered. It knows no color barriers, class distinctions and crosses all economic boundaries to attain its goal

When cupid sends an arrow, even the most hard-hearted crumble weak-kneed to grovel at love's altar. Love makes grown men cry and strong women feel faint. It turns your world upside down and inside out. Once in love's spell, all good sense falls to the wayside and our world, as we have known it, is never again the same.

Those calendars we so meticulously kept might as well be burned. All we then see in each tiny square on each week of every month ahead are little red hearts beside the name of our new love. The brain turns to mush and the heart beats erratically all the time. The only thing we care now about scheduling is our next moment together....preferably alone with one another.

Bob Bamburg, editor of the Alleghany News, offered me the opportunity to write a column for the paper. He asked that I write a bit about myself as an introduction to the readership. I find writing about myself a difficult task.

I am a simple woman. I have traversed no high Andes peaks, invented no disease curing serum, nor broken any world records. I am no more or less special than anyone else. We all plod down the paths of our lives, putting one foot in front of the other getting on down the road of life as best we can. But I can share this with you in case you aren't aware of it....your little corner of western North Carolina is a slice of heaven.

It may appear as a small dot on a large map, but I assure you that there is a kindness to the people here not found everywhere. Y'all probably don't notice it as it envelopes your day to day existence. It is as natural to you as the air you breathe. This atmosphere of mountain community and kindness has brought me home.

I return to North Carolina through a circuitous route of living in several other states. Through the urging of my only son, Nick, I had settled in Richmond, Virginia, but my heart brought me home to North Carolina. My earliest memories are of my granddaddy's farm near here. The feel of the red clay soil squishing between your toes after a rain, water from the well so cold it took your breath away, and the aroma of oiled horse harness in his barn. All those early childhood memories never left me, lurking always in the periphery of my mind. Urging me always to return to what granddaddy called "God's country".

Through the years I traveled here in summer to take my son to camp and in fall just to see the leaves change. Deep in my heart I always knew the mountain siren would lure me home.

Crossing the state line this past month I felt a peacefulness settle over me, a contentment of spirit and happiness in my very soul. I felt the mountain siren smile....I had come home....home to God's country.

❧ ❧ ❧

    I'm not much given to being down and defeated, but only a fool doesn't see when they're well and truly beaten. In this thing, I am…my smartphone has done me in, and I give up. Lt. Colonel Custer and I share a Last Stand. Repeatedly I have tried to learn the fine nuances of this infernal hand held device. Perhaps it is not the technical complexities I find so troublesome and difficult as much as my resistance to trying to grasp it being so great. It seems some great hand in the universe has ordained that these communication devices become the be all and end all of our lives.

    I have a friend who will go back ten miles if her phone is left behind. Can we really not run to the grocery store without it? Will that hour without it significantly matter in the great scheme of life? Is a missed call that important?

    I find it interesting to watch people in restaurants on their devices. So involved are they with their phones that conversation is nearly nonexistent. While waiting to be served in a restaurant when my son was small, we played a spelling game. Going through the alphabet, spelling each word you could think of for each letter, and losing your turn if you couldn't spell a word. It kept him quietly occupied, learning and, most importantly, engaged with me. We were communicating, conversing and laughing. The children I see dining out today barely look up from their phones long enough to order their food.

    I bought the Apple IPhone, gave it my best shot, grew exceedingly irritated and finally went back to my old flip phone. I just want to dial a number if needed and answer when I'm called.

I don't want to calculate my grocery bill, play games, navigate my trip or view my family photos on my cell phone.

I bet folks would be amazed if the hours spent each day looking at their phones could be added up. I mean every glance at the screen, every time it was picked up and toted around, actually used and including the time searching for it. I refuse to allot to that device the precious minutes of what time I have left in each day other than for what is absolutely necessary.

It has become an artificial appendage. Soon it will be implanted behind the ear, and the Big Brother theory could become very real. I can rail against what folks call progress and I won't stop it, but I can refuse to let a device dictate my life. Custer and I both going down fighting against an outcome that we cannot alter and a battle we cannot win.

Intense summer heat had made her stop digging and lean on the shovel handle to rest a moment. A sound made her lift her head and shield her eyes from the sun. Years of habit made her stare down her gravel road. It was a habit borne from years of hope. A mother's kind of hope. The kind that never gives up. Against all odds it steadfastly holds on.

The tiniest wisp of disappointment flickered in her hazel eyes. No, no car was coming….it had never come and probably never would. But hope in a mother's heart springs eternal. Estrangement from your only child was not common in her youth. Today it seems almost as widespread as a plague.

The grim reaper of relationships had swung his scythe clean through her relationship with her son. She had grown so old now and so many years had passed since the split had occurred that she could no longer remember what issues had caused the fracture.

Never a day passed that she didn't think of him, long to see him and to tell him one last time how very much she loved him. He remained her first thought every morning and her last each night. An invisible thread of love binds a mother to her child. A steel cable pales in strength to that thread. No distance can sever its connection. It is a permanent chain of love unlike any other.

Hers was a good life of friends, hobbies and habits that filled all the days that had, in the blink of an eye, turned into years. Life steps in and keeps you busy with its details. The heart glazes over the hurtful hole so you can function, but it never truly heals.

She went back to her thoughts and to digging her flower beds….but wait….was that the sound of tires on gravel….her breath was suspended by the invisible but eternal thread of hope.

Made in the USA
Columbia, SC
06 January 2025

49095644R00119